THE TRADE DEFICIT

ILLEGAL
&
UNCONSTITUTIONAL
EFFECTS

DESTROYING AMERICA

Written For the Layperson

Dr. Alec Feinberg

From the author of the award winning book
<u>The Truth of the Modern Recession</u>
Winner: 2010 Indie Book and USA Book News Finalist Awards
In conjunction with
Citizens For Equal Trade

Publication Date: December 2011

ISBN-13: 9780615497488

ISBN-10: 0615497489

Library of Congress Control Number: 2011936808

For Copyright requests contact the author at
www.TradeDeficitIllegal.com
Printed in the United States of America.

Citizens For Equal Trade (CET)
CET was founded in 2008 to help U.S. citizens, economists, and Congress understand the destructive nature of the trade deficit. We request readers sign our petition at CitizensforEqualTrade.org. We also support the Coalition for a Prosperous America effort and advise readers to join this organization to help fight these trade deficit issues.

Forward

By Peter Crawford, Economy in Crisis

An eye-opening and cogent read, Dr. Feinberg pulls the curtain away from one of America's most undiscussed failings and the corrupt system that enables it. The venomous effects of the trade deficit, as the title suggests, are exposed, explored and condemned. Through a competent use of charts and graphs, Feinberg provides irrefutable, mathematical evidence to support his position on balancing trade. The resulting conclusions hit the reader over the head so blatantly that we are left wondering how anyone is actually allowing these crimes to transpire. The meat of the book is laid out as dynamically as a live presentation that was conducted by the author himself. With less than 150 pages, there is no fluff here: by the second paragraph of the book, Feinberg has already begun measuring the damage with his concise employment of tables and charts. Testimonies from major economists are given discussing the trade deficit's enormous toll on American business. Even without the most basic understanding of foreign economic policy, the reader is easily able to discern why the current system is failing and how it is allowed to do so. Even the sharpest of skeptics will find it terribly difficult to challenge a thesis that is so profoundly backed by facts, figures and logic. But statistics aside, it is the discussion about policy and reform that truly sells this message. Feinberg's passion for his nation's cause leaves a lasting impression that goes beyond left-brained equations and numbers. The corrupt ideology of the global market itself clearly exists: it's presented to us as stone cold as an attorney's playbook. But the reality of its ill effects is what resonates loudest when the last page is turned. This is a perspective that every citizen and legislator needs to examine with real consideration: not because it is our responsibility for what could potentially happen – because it is our responsibility for what has happened already.

By Jerry Wick

This latest book continues the excellent combination of statements followed by detailed verifications first found in "The Truth of The Modern Recession". It's extremely hard to argue with the allegations when the statistical evidence clearly defends the statements. The many charts and graphs take dry data and converts it into something that can be easily and quickly reviewed. The text and illustrations work together and create a compelling combination. Some of the observations might at first seem not to be accurate. The evidence clearly shows the reality behind each statement. Dr.Feinberg also lists his source material so the reader can determine the raw data accuracy. I believe BOTH of Dr. Feinbergs books should be required reading by our congress.

Preface

This book is written for the layperson to help citizens and their representatives understand the economic and financial unjust effects of the U.S. trade deficit. The reader will find that their time is not wasted as the issues are presented in a succinct manner that provides a reasonable amount of facts and data to back up each statement on trade deficit effects. These effects are not simply unjust but likely boarders on unlawful activity. A court like case is presented to help the reader understand the serious nature of these trade deficit effects and also helps the layperson more easily digest the unjust economic facts. There are numerous supportive facts for each accusation, but the book does not try and over burden the reader with every possible available fact, focusing on reasonable key evidence.

The book nicely explains and provide verifications on why the trade deficit effects 1) cause higher national debt due to serious tax losses of outsourced jobs, which impose these tax losses unfairly onto U.S. citizens, 2) cause yearly increases in foreign ownership of U.S assets (where it is projected that in 25 years foreigners will likely own 51% of the U.S. economy), 3) forces corporations to ship jobs and manufacturing abroad, 4) creates a competitive disadvantage for manufacturing in the U.S., 5) creates strong separation of wealth, 6) and supports organized international trading crimes such as currency manipulation, product counterfeiting and other unjust manufacturing problems.

As a solution, the book offers that only balanced trade provides a true competitive advantage and is a very feasible alternative to free trade. Here it is explained that only balance trade can control greed, which is the fundamental cause of much of these unjust trade deficit effects. We explain that balance trade is entirely possible and if we can send a man to the moon, we surely can find a way to have an effective balance trade policy. In order to do this, the book explains the need for political economic reliable tools to help congress persons (mostly lawyers) do proper economic problem solving. Such tools would fill a serious gap in their decision making process. A book written in conjunction with Citizens For Equal Trade to help America realize the true consequences and solutions for the U.S. trade deficit.

THE SEVEN CHARGES

The trade deficit without limits causes the following effects:

Charge 1: Increases the national debt from significant tax losses and therefore ends up taking money from U.S. Citizens who must help pay off this increase

Charge 2: Causes the unjust possibly illegal use of public funds to subsidize importing companies both foreign and domestic due to tax losses which increase the national debt

Charge 3: Causes the unjust possibly illegal use of public funds for the purpose of subsidizing the transition of domestic business to foreign countries due to tax losses

Charge 4: Promotes forms of uncontrollable organized crimes against U.S. Citizens

Charge 5: Results in the possible violation of Article IV, Section IV of the U.S. Constitution, where the federal government has a required duty and obligation to remove foreign invaders from U.S. soil and/or states harmed or threatened by them (this refers to the current financial takeover of U.S. companies and its land by foreigners enabled with trade deficit dollars)

Charge 6: Results in the possible violation of Article 1, Section 9, Clause 5 of the U.S. Constitution, where "No Tax or Duty shall be laid on articles exported from any State."

Charge 7: Results in the violation of the intent of the WTO by allowing import goods to be subjected to a reverse tariff.

These are the charges; we explain each and present the evidence to support our arguments. We explain why balanced trade would prevent most of these effects.

TABLE OF CONTENTS

1

WHO PAYS FOR TRADE DEFICIT EFFECTS?

The trade deficit is the number one economic problem in the U.S. It is far worse than the national debt issue causing effects that are highly unjust, having a reasonable degree of questionable unlawfulness. It is not only responsible for the loss of manufacturing and jobs, but much worse, causes national debt and the irreversible effect of enabling the vast sale of America to foreigners as we will discuss. It creates an unreliable economy because the trade deficit is itself a debt that is paid off in goods, services, U.S. treasuries, land, business acquisitions and so forth. Free trade is highly over priced, now costing over $8.5 trillion along with countless ill effects.

One does not have to be a lawyer to ask – are these effects unjust and possibly illegal?

Table 1-1 Trade Deficit Unjust Issues

Trade Deficit Effects	Accusations	Some Key Costs
Currency Manipulation	Organized International Crime	1. Three to five million Jobs 2. Loss of trillions of dollars of public money to foreign countries 3. Topple U.S. industries
Counterfeit Goods, Patent, Copyright and Trademark Piracy	Organized International Crimes	1. Estimated 7% of all U.S. trade, 2. Taking business and jobs away from U.S. companies
Non Tariff Trade Barriers by foreigners	Organized International Crimes	Taking business away from U.S. companies
High Tax Losses from Job Outsourcing, Corporate Loopholes etc.	Unjust Misuse of Public Funds	Increases National Debt – Americans must pay for lost wages and tax loop holes
The Selling of America to Foreigners	Unjust and Possibly Unconstitutional	America foreign owned in 25 years – a foreign invasion?

1

All these effects are explained here. This is a political economic[1] book for the layperson as it explains the need to promote reliable economic change by helping lawmakers and citizens understand the destructive nature of the trade deficit effects.

U.S. citizens should understand that too many effects of the trade deficit are unjust and are destroying America. Therefore, it should be required by law to implement an alternate policy such as an effective balanced trade policy (see Chapter 9) that could prevent these effects and would not violate world trading policies. The Congressperson needs to understand this rather than continue down a path of large yearly trade deficits that sanction these uncontrollable unjust activities. Free trade economists will have an opportunity to understand that ideology that causes unjust activities is not good economics, no matter the theory. New data are presented to irrefutably show the tragic effects of America's large trade deficit. Finally, this book should provide a somewhat of a legal weapon for trade reformists who have been limited in their abilities to get Congress to balance trade. Laws are here to protect U.S. citizens. However, only Congress can fix our unjust trade problems. It is their sworn duty.

Chapters are organized so as not to waste your time. Chapter 1 presents the key facts to help lay the ground work. Chapter 2 presents a court-like case with seven charges against the trade deficit. After each charge is presented, there is a reference table where the reader may find the evidence in the book to prove that the charges are true. Thus, a reader in reality need only read the first two chapters to understand the unjust claims. After that, one can spend as much time as desired on reviewing the supporting evidence presented in other chapters. Additionally, there is a chapter on explaining free trade (Chapter 12). Chapter 10 explains that a gap exists between economists and politicians. This gap is largely responsible for many U.S. misguided policies, such as free trade. What is needed is political economic tools for problem solving as described in Chapters 10 and 11.

First and foremost, we must ask who pays for these trade deficit effects? Who pays for lost tax revenues increasing the national debt caused by job outsourcing and a dwindling job market from lost U.S. manufacturing; and the fact that America consumes much more that it produces but is highly underemployed? Who pays for the tax breaks for multinational corporations (Chapter 3) all that have increased America's national debt (Chapter 4)? Who will pay for China's currency manipulation[2] that has cost more

---

[1] Economic advice given to the government or public on economic policy to enhance its reliability. Also see Chapter 10 on political economics and reliability economics.

[2] Manipulating currency causes China's goods to be artificially cheaper compared to a U.S. manufacturer giving them a competitive advantage and creates higher U.S. trade deficits and national debt.

than 2 million U.S. jobs (Chapter 6); China's manipulative Value Added Tax (VAT)"[3], trade barriers, and blatant trade violations (see Chapter 6), to gain control over and cripple certain industries which costs U.S. jobs? Who will pay for the gigantic trade deficit of which foreigners now own greater than $8.5 trillion (Chapter 3) more of us than we own of them, enabling the sale of American businesses (now 21% owned by foreigners while employing just 3.7% of Americans) (Chapter 5)? Thus, every penny of the trade deficit equates to some sort of asset loss; who will pay for it? How do we explain to Americans who fought and died for our country that profiteers are allowed to freely trade, to trade our country away (such as the New York Stock Exchange now German owned[4])? How do we explain to Americans that in their back yard is this "Trojan horse"[5] trade deficit allowing for this infiltration of foreign ownership potentially dominated by communist China into our country?

> **Remark 1.1:** *New York Times Reports August 11*: "Flush with capital from its enormous trade surpluses... Chinese banks have poured more than $1 billion into commercial real estate in New York ...diversifying beyond U.S. treasuries..."

Who pays for a country run no longer by "we the people," but by corporations (both domestic and now foreign)? Who pays for the separation of wealth that has increased at a rate of 1% a year over the last 25 years (Chapter 8) while the top 0.1% and 1% of the wealthiest Americans pay taxes at an average rate of just 23%[6] (Chapter 8); a separation of wealth that is increasingly foreign owned due to the trade deficit! Who pays for the most non-unified Congress in the history of the United States with excessive representation by corporate lobbyists? The answer is not blowin' in the wind, it is the disappearing middle class, it is U.S. citizens who will surely lose their land, their entitlements, jobs, and have their taxes raised to help pay off the national debt created in part by the trade deficit and wealthy tax loopholes as this book will prove.

Citizens, of course, also pay for the key net effect of the U.S. trade deficit in job losses. The annual trade deficit average over the last 5 years is about $600 billion per year. Cutting the trade deficit in half to $300 billion would create **5 million new jobs**[7]. For

---

[3] Value added taxes are typically charged to importer and equivalently to the domestic non-importer like a sales tax. However, when China charges this to a U.S. importer and not to their own manufacturers in certain areas, or when they provide selective rebates (Chapter 6), it creates an unfair advantage.

[4] It's official: Germans buy NYSE in $10B deal, February 15, 2011,
http://www.crainsnewyork.com/article/20110215/FREE/110219927

[5] From ancient Greece the *Trojan horse* was a deceptive wooden horse token of peace, but inside were soldiers used to conquer the city of Troy.

[6] www.taxfoundation.org/news/show/250.html

[7] Cutting Trade Gap in Half Would Create Up to 5 Million Jobs, P. Morici, June 2011,
http://www.tradereform.org/2011/06/cutting-trade-gap-in-half-would-create-up-to-5-million-jobs/

example, using simple economic math for an annual U.S. salary of $60,000 would yield:

Remark 1.2: $300 billion trade deficit/$60,000 salary=5 Million Jobs

These job losses will escalate hurting the middle class. This is really a key problem because the middle class are really the ones needed to create jobs and provide government revenue. This is because there is more of a direct relationship between consumers spending and jobs than there is between taxes and job creation. In economic terms, it is circulation of money that is needed for full employment[8]. To add to our problems we have a non-unified government made up with mostly lawyers[9] who are making awkward economic decisions and even ignore their own national debt commissioned studies. They may not realize the consequences of fixing one thing while causing problems elsewhere economically as they use no reliable political economic decision tools (see Chapters 10 and 11) to do problem solving. For example the CEO of PIMCO, the world's largest bond fund stated on the August 2, 2011 debt deal in Washington,

Remark 1.3: "The budget agreement does nothing to restore household and corporate confidence. So unemployment will be higher than it would have been otherwise, growth will be lower than it would be otherwise, and inequality will be worse than it would be otherwise."[10]

Table 1-2 Selected countries' unemployment rate & corresponding trade deficits[11,12,13]

Country	Spain	Greece	Portugal	U.S.	Italy	Canada	Germany	China
Unemp. Rate (2011)	20.9%	15.0%	12.4%	9.1%	8.1%	7.2%	6.0%	4.1%
Trade Def. as a %GDP (2010)	-4.7%	-5.6%	-8.3%	-3.9%	-3.0%	-2.7%	+4.9%	+4.6%

There is no mention of balancing trade for *job creation* in Congress. We provide detailed information that there is a 60% to 70% correlation between a country's unemployment rate and its trade deficit.

This above table shows seven countries with this relationship as a crude example. Chapter 7 provides the actual assessment on 25 countries. In the table, we have selected Spain, Greece, Portugal, and Italy, each with high trade deficits as a percent of their

---

[8] Velocity of Money and employment, example, http://en.wikipedia.org/wiki/Velocity_of_money
[9] About two thirds of the Senate and one third of the house are lawyers (about 50% of congress), http://floppingaces.net/2010/11/03/enough-with-the-lawyers-in-congress-reader-post/, another article claims 45% of congress are lawyers, http://www.scholastic.com/teachers/article/time-change-congress
[10] http://abcnews.go.com/Politics/pimco-ceo-mohamed-el-erian-budget-deal-bring/story?id=14199182
[11] http://en.wikipedia.org/wiki/List_of_sovereign_states_by_current_account_balance
[12] http://en.wikipedia.org/wiki/List_of_countries_by_GDP_(nominal)
[13] http://en.wikipedia.org/wiki/List_of_countries_by_unemployment_rate

GDP (indicated by the negative sign) and correspondingly high unemployment rates. These countries also are in the news as having serious national debt problems. One can compare this to China and Germany with low unemployment and correspondingly trade surpluses and manageable budget debts (see Figures 7-2 and 7-3 in Chapter 7 for best comparisons). We note that high unemployment will add to a country's budget problems. It causes less tax revenue to be generated as the unemployed contribute less to the economy. Also, outsourced jobs cannot generate tax revenue.

We provide studies that show the U.S. trade deficit does cause national debt increases. Many economists now agree that any plan to fix the national debt must include balancing trade (see Chapter 4). Free trade provides opportunities to use many manipulative greed tactics by exporting counties like China to force higher exports to the U.S. while reducing U.S. imports into their country. Most of these trading problems, associated unemployment increases, and resulting national debt increases, would be eliminated with balanced trade (which is far superior to free trade as described in Chapter 9). Yet, our politicians are influenced financially by corporate lobbyists representing outsourcing companies that are seeking more and more tax advantages here and overseas. Such corporations have helped escalate the U.S. corporate revenue problems by lobbying for tax loophole advantages. Corporations contributed just 7% to all government revenue collected in 2010 (compared to 20% in 1965)[14]. Politicians support multinational tax breaks to corporations (who help their political campaigns) on blind faith that they will create jobs. This causes lost government revenue, and the awarded tax breaks are not even tied to job creation. In fact, more jobs are created overseas with these tax breaks and loopholes. This is apparent since 83 of the largest 100 U.S. companies have overseas tax havens, and there are 19,000 corporations incorporated into one single P.O. address in the Cayman Islands[15,16].

> **Remark 1.4:** "According to the Government Accountability Office, 57% of U.S. companies doing business in the U.S. paid no federal income taxes for at least one year from 1998 to 2005. For example, in 2009 GE, Bank of America, Citigroup, and Valero did not pay any taxes on their income."[17] ...A comprehensive study released on Nov. 3, 2011, found that 280 of the biggest publicly traded American companies faced federal income tax bills equal to 18.5 percent of their profits dur-

---

[14] See Chapter 3, Figure 3-1

[15] http://messageboards.aol.com/aol/en_us/articles.php?boardId=87893&articleId=610761&func=6&channel=People+Connection&filterRead=false&filterHidden=true&filterUnhidden=false

[16] http://finance.yahoo.com/blogs/daily-ticker/corporate-america-pays-lot-less-taxes-think-125020207.html#ixzz1TvF94h2U

[17] The Real State of America Atlas, Cynthia Enloe, Joni Seager

ing the last three years — little more than half the official corporate rate of 35 percent and lower than their competitors in many industrialized countries[18]...

It is as if politicians keep passing legislation to help increase the trade deficit, reduce government revenues (thereby hurting the national debt), force corporations to compete with outsourcing, and are enabling China and foreigners to financially take over the U.S. causing a perfect storm (see Operation Trade Deficit, Section 1.3.1). These reasons and job losses to China and NAFTA have caused 70% of Americans to now oppose free trade[19]. Without trade reform, we will likely end up in a "double dip recession, or worse"[20], including losing control of America to foreign ownership.

Free trade is broken and way out of control, countries follow China's example and now violate our trade agreements daily (with numerous taxes and other clever schemes) to gain excessive competitive advantages to win U.S. dollars. These are organized crimes that include trade violations of currency manipulation, foreign product subsidies, non-tariff trade barriers, U.S. intellectual property rights, product counterfeiting, etc. (see Chapter 6). Each of these increases the U.S. trade deficit, ends up in some manner, hurting U.S. companies, costs jobs, creating lost tax revenues, and adds to the U.S. national debt. Only balanced trade can stop all these effects.

There is little hope that free trade's train wreck, the trade deficit, can be stopped in time by today's non-unified Congress. Possibly a threat of a court case should prompt congressional action on the trade deficit. We should not allow a policy on unlimited yearly trade deficits that supports unjust activities to continue. Leaving the trade deficit as is:

- Creates massive tax revenue losses that keep adding to our national debt
- Supports a foreign invasion into our country that is quickly gaining ownership over our land and businesses
- Creates high unemployment
- Creates separation of wealth and loss of the middle class
- Will continue to transfer U.S. wealth to foreigners
- Supports high organized trading crimes

For example, what we mean by a foreign invasion is that foreigners now own 21% of America's businesses (enabled with U.S. trade deficit profits) and foreigners are in the process of taking control of America. Meanwhile, foreign controlled U.S. businesses proportionally only employs U.S. citizens at a rate of about 3.7% (see Chapter 5). New

---

[18] http://www.nytimes.com/2011/11/03/business/280-big-public-firms-paid-little-us-tax-study-finds.html
[19] www.cnbc.com/id/39407846/53_in_US_Say_Free_Trade_Hurts_Nation_NBC_WSJ_Poll
[20] Avoiding a Double Dip Recession, or Worse, P. Morci, June 2011,
http://www.tradereform.org/2011/06/avoiding-a-double-dip-recession-or-worse/

facts will show that foreigners are projected to own 51% of U.S. businesses in less than 25 years and this could bankrupt our economy with skyrocketing unemployment (i.e. foreigners do not employ enough Americans). This is what we term America's Trojan Horse trade deficit. Facts here support all the above claims. Only understanding this injustice might persuade Congress to balance or limit the amount of trade deficit.

The trade deficit's long-term effects are not easy to understand. Even most economists are conflicted with free trade ideology. However, Congress is sworn to uphold the constitution and the law. Legislatures can no longer turn a blind eye to these unjust and possibly illegal issues. Once legislatures understand that a trade deficit without limits is in fact resulting in continual unjust activities, they must act. Putting the trade deficit into layperson's legal terms is important as it simplifies the issues and puts the facts into a less debatable light. After all, most Congress members are lawyers, are sworn to uphold the law, and are more comfortable understanding the issues this way. Economists will have an opportunity to understand that ideology that is unfair is not good economics, no matter their theories.

1.1 What is the U.S. Trade Deficit Policy?
The basic concepts of free trade and the trade deficit are provided in Chapter 12, Appendix 2 to aid the reader who would like an informative overview.

Here we briefly describe some important basics principles and overview U.S. trade deficit policy. The U.S. has a policy of free trade, which means that between U.S. trading partners, (for most goods and services) there are no tariffs so trading is free across borders in accordance with the World Trade Organization (WTO) agreement. U.S. companies can sell products overseas and foreign companies can sell products in the U.S. ideally for most products without tariffs. When America buys more import products from foreigners than we export and sell to them, this creates a trade deficit. Of course, there is no WTO agreement that says the U.S. cannot seek to balance its trade. However, trading deficits have in fact occurred in the U.S. since 1971. These deficits have escalated since the signing of the North American Free Trade Agreement (NAFTA) in December 1993 and China's entrance into the U.S. marketplace in October 2000 (see Chapter 12, Appendix 2). The total U.S. trade deficit by the end of 2011 reached $8.5 trillion, of which $6.5 trillion occurred in just the last 12 years.

U.S. Trade Deficit Policy is in fact rooted in free trade policy. There is currently no limit on the allowance of how much a yearly U.S. trade deficit can be. In 2006, a record U.S. trade deficit occurred of $0.76 trillion. In the last 10 years (2001-2010) the yearly trade deficit has averaged well over a half trillion dollars ($0.56 trillion). These are astronomical world record amounts that no economist (not even free trade founders) can defend. Many countries feel that America's trade policy is the laughing stock of the world. America has the largest national debt and largest trade deficit. These two facts are somewhat connected, as we demonstrate, and are root cause underlying failure problems of our economy.

There are many effects of the trade deficit that we will discuss. The primary effect of allowing these deficits to occur is loss of U.S. manufacturing and jobs. The main contributors to the trade deficit are rising oil prices and imports of non oil goods primarily from China. The trade deficit also comes from areas that people do not realize, such as the U.S. sports trade deficit occurring in golf and baseball in which foreign athletes make excessive (under-taxed) dollars, far greater than American athletes make abroad. Allowing the trade deficit to be without limits has shown to be highly destructive behavior for the U.S. economy. Most of the unfair activities that we discuss are related to the trade deficit of goods (not oil). However, both create foreign wealth and loss of U.S. assets, which leads to harsh problems as well. This will soon become clearer.

1.1.1 What Does it Mean to Limit the Trade Deficit?

When we talk of limiting the trade deficit we mean requiring trade to be balanced to a reasonable amount. We would like to see the trade deficit, over a reasonable adjustment time period, start to be limited and slowly be reduced to almost zero. Often economists quantify things in terms of percent of our annual Gross Domestic Product (GDP). GDP is used as it is the best measure of our economy's performance each year. It measures the market value of all final goods and services produced within a country on an annual basis. Here is one example of how balanced trade might start.

> **Remark 1.5:** *Oct. 2010: "Treasury Secretary Tim Geithner proposed a new trade plan to the G-20 meeting (our free trade meeting with other countries). The idea is to limit national current account balances (i.e. the trade deficit) to a hard cap of **4% annual Gross Domestic Product (GDP)**."*[21]

We see Geithner had good intentions to limiting the trade deficit's size. Yet later in March, Geithner backed off under pressure from China.

> **Remark 1.6:** *March 2011: In testimony before the Senate Foreign Relations Committee on March 2, U.S. Treasury Secretary Timothy Geithner explained why he thinks that market forces will balance U.S.-China trade without the Obama administration having to do anything more than talk."*[22]

---

[21] www.economicpopulist.org/content/us-treasury-secretary-geithner-proposes-balanced-trade
[22] http://seekingalpha.com/article/256558-geithner-thinks-u-s-trade-issues-with-china-are-solving-themselves

As a measure of Geithner's initial plan to see if it was a good target, we note that in 2010, the trade deficit was about $0.5 trillion dollars (about 3.8% of GDP) of which half of this was due to oil imports (1.9% of GDP). Even Geithner's original proposal would not have limited the 2010 trade deficit.

1.1.2 Euro and Dollar Free Trade Violation Cost Millions of Jobs & Global Crisis

One additional concept of free trade that is imperative for the reader to understand is the concept of money circulation amongst countries. Here we refer to the key principle of free trade that currency must find its way back to the country of origin. For example, in the U.S. when a Chinese company receives U.S. dollars for their sale of goods, these dollars must eventually find its way back to the U.S. since in China, the yuan is their currency. Thus, the Chinese company may exchange the dollars to a bank in China for yuans, but eventually that bank will reinvest those dollars back in the U.S., perhaps in U.S. treasuries, investing or taking control of U.S. companies, or real-estate, etc.

Sometimes this principle is not respected in a country's monetary policy. The creation of the Euro itself is a major violation of this principle and an overlooked problem in Europe for trade deficit countries like Italy, Greece, Spain and Portugal with their debt crises[23]. Many countries trade throughout Europe as well as China and the U.S. When China receives Euros from Greece for example, they must reinvest them somewhere. However, with the Euro system, they do not have to return this money to the country of origin and these Euros can be reinvested anywhere in Europe. The wise choice is to reinvest those Euros in a country that is more solvent like Germany and not return the money back to Greece. Thus it is likely that the insolvent countries do not see much of their trade deficit Euros back. And this is a key overlooked problem to the European financial crisis. Therefore, the Euro ends up being redistributed to the solvent countries leaving the insolvent countries like Greece and Spain with fewer and fewer Euros invested in their economies.

This is no small matter. For example, Portugal, Greece, Spain, and Italy have had typical trade deficits ranging from 3 to 10 percent of each county's GDP, depending on the year. If this money is rarely reinvested back into these countries, over say a 15 year period, it can add up in substantial Euro losses of the order of magnitude of a country's GDPs and significantly reduce their working capital, hurt the circulation of money needed to sustain job growth, and increase their debt problems. Meanwhile the Euros may end up say in the German economy, but the crisis drags down the value of this cur-

---

[23] Free Trade Violation is a Major Cause of Euro Crisis, A. Feinberg, September 2011, www.economyincrisis.org/content/free-trade-violation-major-cause-euro-crisis

rency and all countries lose. However, right now, Greece is the biggest loser and will likely default soon on their debt. The only solution at this point may be to unify Europe similar to the U.S. or go back to Europe's prior monetary system. While there are many economists discussing the European debt crisis, we have not heard any mention of this key issue which must be part of their solution.

In the U.S., there is also a similar violation of the free trade reinvestment principle due to one of its tax codes. For multinational corporations, cash earned abroad stays abroad due to a deferred taxation allowance passed by congress that foolishly allows U.S. companies to keep U.S. dollars abroad. If it were brought back, it would be subject to corporate tax that can cost as much as 35 percent. The result, according to *The New York Times* [1], an estimated \$1.375 trillion is being held outside the U.S. by 519 American multinational companies. This tax law violates this principle of free trade as well, since money is not returning to the country of origin, the U.S., in a timely manner. And there is no incentive to return the money to the U.S. The results: increases in the national debt due to tax losses, losses in U.S. investment to create jobs, and other related loss of employment (because money needs circulate to create employment). Just 10% of this money would create over 2 million jobs. For example, using our simple economic math for an annual U.S. salary of \$60,000 would yield:

Remark 1.7: \$1.375 trillion/\$60,000 salary x 10%=2.29 Million Jobs

This is entirely possible as loss of government taxes equates to government job losses never mind the possibility that this money might be used by companies to invest in U.S. job growth activities. Here we have explained that this simple violation of free trade reinvestment principle is costing millions of global jobs and part of the global crisis.

1.2 Evidence on Unjust Trade Deficit Effects Destroying America

Fact 1: We present economic statistical studies along with easy to understand explanations of how a key effect of the trade deficit is to create significant national debt (primarily due to lost taxes from unemployment and multinational corporate tax breaks). These findings are recent and detailed in Chapters 3 and 4 with logical and statistical evidence. Now more than ever before, as Democrats and Republicans in 2011 try to reduce the national debt through major program cuts and raising taxes, we must realize that a portion of this national debt is due to the trade deficit. And if the national debt increases even more due to the trade deficit, Americans have to pay for this extra debt as well. Another way to think of this is that we are being forced to pay for the trade deficit effects through increases in our taxes and loss of our entitlements. This creates an unjust situation and can be considered taking money from hard working families across America because of the trade deficit. It means companies that sell U.S. imports, both foreign and domestic, are being subsidized by the average American who will pay this trade deficit tax. <u>This trade deficit tax is a serious misuse of public funds</u>.

It is difficult to justify a trade deficit policy without limits. The excessive Chinese imports that so dominate our trade deficit should be our first major reduction goal to balance trade (see Chapter 9). The portion of the trade deficit caused by oil imports also needs to be addressed in America's energy policy. For example, the U.S. has more than enough natural gas to markedly reduce its foreign oil dependence. It is really unforgivable that our government does not use natural gas vehicles (see petition on natural gas vehicles[24]), for example, to start helping this process, yet subsidizes far less productive energy programs[25].

Fact 2: Our trade policy creates uncontrollable job and product outsourcing and factory offshoring. Product outsourcing and factory offshoring create imports that become part of our trade deficit. As a result, there is a reduction in manufacturing and job losses. This creates taxable revenue shortages. Companies' offshoring provide less tax revenues due to new tax loopholes and tax advantages in producing products overseas. This is in fact a root cause of the trade deficit tax issue discussed in Fact 1. This tax loss is unfair as it ends up passing larger and larger bills along to U.S. citizens through increases to the national debt as discussed in Fact 1.

Fact 3: The trade deficit encourages and creates highly uncontrollable organized trading crimes supporting foreign cheating. Try as they might, U.S. government and customs cannot keep up with all import trade violations. A key organized crime by China and Japan that is well known is currency manipulation. This and other activities are detailed in Chapter 6. U.S. corporations consistently lose billions of dollars in intellectual property every year due to patent, copyright, trademark piracy infringements, product counterfeiting, product subsidies, hidden foreign trade barriers, manipulative import VAT tax (see Chapter 6) irregularities, and violations in foreign anti-dumping agreements, and so forth. Currency manipulation itself is shown to have cost at least 2 million American jobs (see Chapter 6). It is also believed that about 7% of all global trade is related to counterfeit goods. Even many Chinese companies' stock values are falsely inflated profiteers to steal investor's

---

[24] https://wwws.whitehouse.gov/petitions/%21/petition/mandate-new-us-gov-usps-vehicles-be-natural-gas-powered/1n2WF4H0?utm_source=wh.gov&utm_medium=shorturl&utm_campaign=shorturl
[25] www.dallasnews.com/business/energy/20110330-obama-endorses-pickens-plan-for-natural-gas-vehicles.ece, http://murphy.house.gov/index.cfm?sectionid=44&sectiontree=23,24,44&itemid=1190

money[26]. China turns a blind eye to cheating as it brings dollars to their country. There is no doubt that China has actively gone after and crippled numerous U.S. manufacturing industries with subtle methods that violate WTO policy through product dumping, subsidies, and manipulative VAT taxes to gain dominance. The Steel[27] and Green Industry (Solar and Wind[28]) are two good examples.

> **Remark 1.8:** *Oct. 19, 2011 "...A group of seven U.S. solar panel companies filed a federal trade complaint against Chinese companies they accuse of "dumping" solar products on global markets to depress prices... China is unfairly subsidizing its industries....Those struggles were underscored by the collapse in Solyndra LLC. The solar panel maker based in Fremont, Calif., was the beneficiary of a half-billion-dollar federal loan but filed for bankruptcy in August and laid off its 1,100 workers....* "[29]
>
> *"...The bankruptcies of three American <u>solar power</u> companies in the last month...have left China's industry with a dominant sales position..."*[30]

> **Remark 1.9:** *"...But China's government has subsidized the creation of a large steel industry that is now exporting big amounts of cut-price steel to the United States, said Andrew Sharkey, president of the American Iron & Steel Institute. Those subsidies, including discounted prices for land and energy, low-cost loans and debt forgiveness, represent unfair trading practices that threaten the U.S. industry, he said...***The U.S. steel industry can compete against other companies, he said, but "we can't compete against other governments."*** The AISI represents 31 steel makers..."*[31]

These violations are not just in the U.S.[32] The trade wars and crimes not only create lost jobs but force American companies to go bankrupt. This results in lost jobs and corporate problems and also adds up to huge losses in badly needed government revenues causing higher national debt. This increased debt and robs every U.S. taxpayer. It is a

---

[26] http://finance.yahoo.com/blogs/daily-ticker/invasion-chinese-reverse-mergers-under-attack-josh-brown-121928402.html

[27] http://www.solarserver.com/solar-magazine/solar-news/current/kw38/us-files-wto-cases-against-china-including-case-over-us-steel-export-dispute.html

[28] http://www.portlandtribune.com/news/story.php?story_id=128579295581531200

[29] http://finance.yahoo.com/news/US-solar-firms-file-trade-apf-76123229.html?x=0&sec=topStories&pos=7&asset=&ccode=

[30] http://www.nytimes.com/2011/09/02/business/global/us-solar-company-bankruptcies-a-boon-for-china.html?_r=1&ref=energy-environment

[31] http://www.nytimes.com/2007/09/19/business/worldbusiness/19iht-steel.4.7570304.html

[32] http://www.theaustralian.com.au/news/opinion/chinas-free-trade-cheating-threatens-our-jobs/story-e6frg6zo-1226007170647

serious form of organized crime across our country and can only be stopped by requiring politicians to balance trade (see Chapter 9).

The U.S.' largest importer, China, has proven itself to be a highly dishonest trading partner (see Chapter 6). In theory, China owes America trillions of dollars from their trading crimes. The U.S. Congress is in fact having quite a difficult time in figuring out what to do about their currency manipulation[33]. As a potential manufacturer, you should think twice about working with a dishonest trading country that is demonstrating serious trading crimes of aggression against the U.S.A. Certainly there are more honest manufacturing countries that you should consider.

Table 1-3 Summary of Facts on why the trade deficit cost tax payer money

1.	The trade deficit means Americans are buying more products made by foreigners rather than products made by Americans.
2.	Cheaper labor encourages U.S. companies to manufacture outside the U.S. mostly in China. These imports create much of our trade deficit.
3.	U.S. government cannot collect taxes from foreign employees.
4.	Therefore, the trade deficit causes lost U.S. government taxes.
5.	Lost taxes occur not just from displaced U.S. jobs, but from lost manufacturing, tax loopholes for multinational corporations, foreign cheating, China's currency manipulation, product counterfeiting …etc.).
6.	Each of these causes tax losses, i.e., less money that the U.S. government can collect.
7.	These government tax losses create more national debt.
8.	These logical arguments and statistical studies now verify that a trade deficit effect is to increase the national debt.
9.	Americans get the bill for the extra national debt caused by the trade deficit effect.
10.	Therefore the trade deficit is causing higher taxes for Americans and forcing the government to make new spending cuts that would have benefited Americans.
11.	This is unjust use of public funds to cause new taxes due to trade policy. It is like taking money from Americans' wallets to force them to pay new taxes due to these trade deficit effects. Why should any American have to pay more taxes to help trade activities?
12.	Balanced trade would not create these problems.

Fact 4: Foreign Invasion - The trade deficit passed the $8.5 trillion mark at the end of 2011. This statement can be viewed to mean 1) As of this date, foreigners owned $8.5 trillion more of us than we do of them and 2) foreigners are slowly gaining control of our wealth and our business assets (creating more separation of U.S. wealth to foreign-

---

[33] http://faircurrency.org/legislation.html

ers) and allowing for a new type of foreign invasion. Thus the trade deficit is really similar to a national debt, every trade deficit dollar cost citizens some form of loss, typically in the sale of U.S. treasuries, the sale of U.S. businesses, or its land. Thus, the trade deficit equates to selling off America piece by piece to foreigners. Corporations are the enablers of the trade; they take profits from trade deficit goods, while Americans end up losing jobs and their country.

At first it may appear illogical to view this as a source for foreign invasion. Let's make this a bit clearer. Foreigners now own over 21% of all revenue-bearing U.S. businesses. They are projected to own 51% of all U.S. revenue bearing businesses in under 25 years (see Chapter 5). Greater than 50% is regarded in the corporate world as legal ownership and a controlling interest. Since we are all shareholders in America, at what point do we ask the unthinkable question, "If foreigners own 51% of America, than do Americans still own and control their country"? If your answer is no, i.e. Americans will not be able to own or control their own country, than you must come to the inevitable conclusion that the country will essentially be owned and controlled by foreign governments without a bullet being fired. If this is the case, then we have a foreign invasion underway. This will become clearer in Chapter 5. The reality is our country's leaders are losing control of the political-economic interest in America.

1.3.1 Operation Trade Deficit– Plan for a Foreign Takeover

The reader is now in a position to understand that we could not design a more perfect plan to help foreigners gain financial control over the United States than Operation Trade Deficit. This book will show that Operation Trade Deficit includes: 1) The transfer on average of over a half a trillion trade deficit dollars from the U.S. to foreigners each year (mostly to China) enabled by corporate profiteers, 2) foreigners then reinvesting that money by purchasing U.S. treasuries and taking control of U.S. businesses, its commercial real estate, thereby driving the U.S. deeper into debt, 3) strengthening the foreigners' position while they transfer U.S. jobs and businesses to their countries, 4) U.S. companies are also forced to outsource jobs to compete, 4) foreign owned domestic companies and domestic owned companies enlist corporate lobbyists in Washington to lobby for their multinational tax breaks (see Chapter 3), which accelerates foreign ownership and increases America's national debt, - passing these lost revenues onto U.S. citizens. All these events happening without any bullets being fired on the battle field, leaving America's military helpless to the fact that foreigners are now gaining financial control over America, putting the only hope of stopping this in the hands of politicians who have been bought by multinational corporations: a congress that does not understand the implications of Operation Trade Deficit.

1.4 Trade Deficit Effects Violates the Intent of the WTO

Fact 5: The WTO (World Trade Organization) intent is to eliminate tariffs amongst trading countries. Yet the trade deficit, as it is explained in Chapters 3 and 4, has the effect of causing national debt increases, which means citizens effectively pay a trade deficit tax. A tax on goods is considered a tariff. Because this is a tax we pay on imports as the buyer, it is in reverse. Normally, if there is a tax it is paid by the exporting country, not the people receiving the goods. We can then interpret that tax as a "reverse tariff." The agreement between our trading partners requires elimination of tariffs and quotas on most (if not all) goods and services traded between them. Since the trade deficit effect creates a "reverse tariff," it violates the intent of the WTO Free Trade Policy!

1.5 Educational Trade Deficit – Subsidized Colleges Favor Foreign Students

We briefly mention the educational trade deficit since it is a totally unrecognizable unethical behavior by subsidized U.S. colleges. Here we refer to the fact that U.S. colleges and graduate schools, are now providing degrees to foreigners, at an exceedingly high rate, motivated by receiving larger tuition fees[34] from foreigners, effectively selling out American students, who get bumped to lower ranking schools, and often cannot later compete for good paying jobs[35, 36, 37, 38]. For example studies found:

Remark 1.10: *"Of the 2006 doctoral degrees, 15,459 were American citizens, while 12,775 were not citizens. In some fields, notably computer sciences and engineering, foreign-born students already make up more than 60% of graduates"[39]*

Remark 1.11: In 2009, *"International students currently comprise about 15.5% of all students at U.S. graduate schools"[40,41] In 2010 there were 411,000 student visas issued[42], and in 2009 there were 3,205,000 college degrees awarded[43]. Therefore we estimate that about 12.8% of all college students are foreigners.*

---

[34] http://scccstudentnews.wordpress.com/2010/11/11/international-students-pay-higher-tuition-fees/

[35] http://chronicle.com/article/Number-of-Foreign-Students-in/49142/

[36] http://nces.ed.gov/pubs98/web/98042.asp

[37] http://chronicle.com/article/Graduate-School-Applications/127086/

[38] www.stanford.edu/dept/presprovost/irds/ir/analytical_reports/stats_book/1.6_Percent_Foreign_Students.pdf

[39] http://blog.chron.com/sciguy/2007/11/by-2010-most-science-ph-d-s-will-go-to-foreign-born-students/

[40] Bell, N. 2010. *Graduate Enrollment and Degrees: 1999 to 2009*. Washington, DC: Council of Graduate Schools.

[41] http://www.cgsnet.org/portals/0/pdf/R_IntlApps11_I.pdf

[42] http://en.wikipedia.org/wiki/F_visa

[43] http://www.census.gov/compendia/statab/2012/tables/12s0299.pdf

To make matters worse, U.S. citizens are funding this educational trade deficit through property tax relief to these colleges[44] and government grants. These graduate students end up taking away high paying jobs from Americans making even higher salaries. In fact, studies find foreign technology workers using H1B visas and green cards in the United States are making premium wages[45] and later return with their U.S. job saving dollars to their foreign countries. Often employers claim that qualified U.S. candidates are unavailable. We believe this is in large part due to this lack of educational opportunity for American students. Colleges pay little, if any, property tax, also are awarded research grants for graduate programs, and then turn around and show poor loyalty to your sons or daughters when they apply to American undergraduate or graduate schools, potentially rejecting them in favor of a foreign student for higher tuition fees. Many of these foreign students pay for U.S. education with trade deficit dollars. This foreign wealth also drives up the cost of a U.S. college education, flooding our schools with admission requests. The property taxes are sacrificed revenues by towns and cities across America in order to help partially subsidize American students. And government grants are a major source of revenue for University research graduate programs. The reality is, much of this money subsidizes foreign education. The results: a less competitive U.S. with tax dollars helping foreigners while a large percentage of U.S. students end up rejected at the school of their choice because a foreign student was accepted in their place and later graduated and took away an American job on visa status. Meanwhile, you are forced to pay taxes to subsidize this yearly scenario. While this activity may not be illegal by schools, it certainly should be required of colleges to have reasonable foreign student quotas with visa restrictions on graduates so that they do not take away jobs.

1.6 What Should and Can be Done for the Trade Deficit?

It is clear that the trade deficit should have reasonable limits and plans need to be made to work to have an effective balance trade policy. If we can send a man to the moon, we surely can find a way to balance trade. The only reasonable way to do this is with good economic problem solving tools as we propose in Chapters 10 and 11. There are key trade deficit areas that must be reduced as we have stated: 1) oil imports and 2) imports of (non oil) goods mostly from China. We briefly discussed that oil imports can be highly reduced by using natural gas[46]. There are currently no such common sense U.S.

---

[44]http://host.madison.com/news/local/education/campus_connection/article_0d580b02-7a8b-11e0-99ae-001cc4c03286.html

[45] H-1B Workers Earn More Than U.S. Workers, Finds Study, www.eweek.com/c/a/IT-Management/H1B-Workers-Earn-More-Than-US-Workers-Finds-Study-365625/?kc=EWKNLCSM05252010STR1

[46] http://murphy.house.gov/index.cfm?sectionid=44&sectiontree=23,24,44&itemid=1190

energy policies. Second, not seeking to control imports from China really is highly destructive U.S. behavior. We demonstrate that this results in highly unjust effects (likely illegal and unconstitutional). There have been a number of ignored proposals to balance trade (see Chapter 9). The most famous is the 2006 Warren Buffett proposal to balance trade using import certificates[47] (see Chapter 9). There are certainly many options to balance trade that should be considered. Whatever the method to equalize trade, the reader should be reminded that seeking to balance trade does not violate WTO policy.

1.7 What Would Balanced Trade Do?

Balanced trade would:

- Eliminate further increases in the national debt due to the trade deficit
- Help to balance the budget through increased revenues
- Eliminate company offshoring tax loop holes
- Eliminate the trade deficit tax (reverse tariff)
- Stop encouraging outsourcing and offshoring
- Stop encouraging foreign cheating (currency manipulation, product counterfeiting, product subsidies, hidden foreign trade barriers, etc.)
- Stop forcing the foreign financial invasion and foreign ownership of the U.S. economy
- Reduce separation of wealth

Besides the fact that the trade deficit produces unjust effects, there is one other reason why a Congressperson should seek to balance trade, and that is public opinion. Any candidate who has the courage to stand up against free trade would win his election by a landslide since public opinion is now highly negative on free trade.

Remark 1.12: *"September 2010: NBC News/Wall Street Journal Poll [48] showed that 69 percent of Americans believe free trade agreements with other countries have cost jobs in the United States, while just 18 percent believe they have created jobs. A 53 percent majority—up from 46 percent three years ago and 30 percent in 1999—believes that trade agreements have hurt the nation overall....While 65 percent of union members say free trade has hurt the U.S., ... Democratic pollster Peter Hart and his Republican counterpart Bill McInturff, who conduct the NBC/WSJ poll, say the greatest shift against free trade has come among relatively affluent Americans, or those earning more than $75,000 a year."*

---

[47] http://en.wikipedia.org/wiki/Import_Certificates
[48] www.cnbc.com/id/39407846/53_in_US_Say_Free_Trade_Hurts_Nation_NBC_WSJ_Poll

Most Americans are really fed up with free trade policy. They do not want it. This book provides supporting facts that such public opinion is also technically right, since the effect of free trade is that it ends up creating massive trade deficit effects, which are unjust and morally wrong. Any member of Congress, who turns a blind eye to the facts presented here, is simply not obeying the oath of office. If you are a Congress member, it is your sworn oath to uphold the law and constitution. You must seek to balance U.S. trade. Congress should support corporate America in the right way. Congress should not allow our country to be sold piece by piece and make Americans subsidize the sale. Americas have died building and defending our country. Now the battlefield has shifted. The battle can only be fought and won by our Congress. It is time for Congress to defend our country with their pens from this foreign invasion that is robbing Americans of their ownership and future. It is time for all legislatures to have the courage to wage this battle and face up to the trade deficit before it is too late or America will soon fall like the Roman Empire.

1.8 Unbalanced Trade Deindustrialization Facts

Some Key Facts that have occurred in America's large unbalanced trade deficit that has caused deindustrialization[49]:

1) The United States has lost approximately 42,400 factories since 2001.[50]
2) The United States has lost a total of about 3 to 5.5 million manufacturing jobs since October 2000.[51]
3) In 1959, manufacturing represented 28% of U.S. economic output. In 2008, it represented 11.5%.[52]
4) From 1999 to 2008, employment at the foreign affiliates of U.S. parent companies increased an astounding 30% to 10.1 million.[53]
5) At the end of 2010 foreigners owned 21% of all U.S. revenue-bearing businesses and are projected to own 51% of them in fewer than 25 years and anticipated to cause skyrocketing U.S. unemployment (Chapter 5).
6) America is being sold off, for example, Germans recently purchased and took control of the U.S. N.Y. Stock exchange[54] by Destsche Borse!
7) Currency manipulation cost 2.1 of 3 million lost trade deficit jobs.[55]

---

[49] www.businessinsider.com/deindustrialization-factory-closing-2010-9#the-united-states-has-lost-approximately-42400-factories-since-2001-1

[50] prospect.org/cs/articles?article=the_plight_of_american_manufacturing

[51] prospect.org/cs/articles?article=the_plight_of_american_manufacturing

[52] prospect.org/cs/articles?article=the_plight_of_american_manufacturing

[53] taxprof.typepad.com/files/128tn1102.pdf

[54] It's official: Germans buy NYSE in $10B deal, February 15, 2011, http://www.crainsnewyork.com/article/20110215/FREE/110219927

[55] www.economyincrisis.org/content/currency-manipulation-cost-21-3-million-lost-trade-deficit-jobs-0

8) The United States has lost 32% of its manufacturing jobs since the year 2000.[56]

9) Manufacturing employment in the U.S. computer industry was lower in 2010 than it was in 1975.[57]

10) The Census Bureau says 43.6 million Americans are now living in poverty, which is the highest number of poor Americans in 51 years that records have been kept.[58]

11) In 2008, 1.2 billion cell phones were sold worldwide; none of these were manufactured inside the United States.[59]

12) Dell announced (Sept. 2010) plans to dramatically expand its operations in China with an investment of over $100 billion over the next decade.[60]

13) Dell announced (Sept. 2010) that it will be closing its last large U.S. manufacturing facility in North Carolina. Approximately 900 jobs will be lost.[61]

14) Ford Motor Company announced (Aug. 2010) the closure of a factory that produces the Ford Ranger in St. Paul, Minnesota; approximately 750 good paying middle class jobs are going to be lost.[62]

In the world of free trade – the theory of "comparative advantage"[63] is one of greed. It is really a design flaw of free trade. As a simple analogy, we note that automakers design cars to fight the environment, protecting cars from rust and heat damage. Yet U.S. free trade policy is one that is not designed to fight its biggest environment threat: that of greed. As the reader will soon learn, lack of this protection, such as simply requiring balanced trade, leads to high trading crimes.

Congress currently has no strategies today to balance the trade deficit and stop deindustrialization. While thousands of articles[64] and cries from trade reformists continue, it appears it might take related legal action to cause this Congress to act. The key reason for writing this book is to provide a legal like case that will promote Congress to stop the unjust U.S. trade policy.

---

[56] prospect.org/cs/articles?article=the_plight_of_american_manufacturing

[57] www.businessweek.com/magazine/content/10_28/b4186048358596.htm

[58] www.washingtonpost.com/wp-dyn/content/article/2010/09/16/AR2010091602698_pf.html

[59] prospect.org/cs/articles?article=the_plight_of_american_manufacturing

[60] content.dell.com/us/en/corp/d/secure/2010-09-16-chengdu.aspx

[61] www.statesman.com/business/technology/dell-plans-second-large-manufacturing-center-in-china-920959.html

[62] www.economyincrisis.org/content/american-factories-continue-shutter

[63] A situation in which a country or region can produce a good at a lower opportunity cost than a competitor. This is part of free trade theory.

[64] www.tradereform.org

2

THE COURT CASE AGAINST TRADE DEFICIT POLICY

This book provides a court-like case against the U.S. Trade Deficit Policy which allows no limits on its size. We make the case with supporting facts from many sources. The case is presented in a layperson's legal terms to emphasize the unjust nature of the trade deficit effects. Whether these or similar charges could be proven in a court of law is not necessarily the point. It is relevant to demonstrate the unjust and unfair nature of the trade deficit's effect which in a common sense view, borders on unlawful activities.

Please note for the interested reader, Chapter 12, Appendix 2, provides an overview of free trade basics. The reader may wish to peruse this chapter before reading on.

2.1: The Case Against the U.S. Trade Deficit – Opening Arguments and Charges

As a reader of this book, we invite you to be a member of the jury as we present our case against the U.S. trade deficit. We briefly explained in Chapter 1 that there are no legal limits on how large a yearly U.S. trade deficit can amount to or accumulate to over the years. The trade deficit is primarily due to imports of oil as well as goods from China. The U.S. should minimally first balance the trade deficit from (non oil) goods. Like the national debt, which Congress is trying to reduce for fear of the economic consequences, a trade deficit policy without limits also has powerful economic consequences that are destroying the U.S. economy by the selling of its assets. You will hear evidence and supporting facts to this effect. Here we summarize seven charges claiming the trade deficit without limits causes the following effects:

Charge 1: Increases the national debt from significant tax losses and therefore ends up unjustly <u>taking money from U.S. Citizens</u> who must help pay off this increase

Charge 2: <u>Causes the unjust and possibly illegal use of public funds to subsidize importing companies both foreign and domestic</u> due to tax losses which increase the national debt

Charge 3: <u>Causes the unjust and possibly illegal use of public funds for the purpose of subsidizing the transition of domestic business to foreign countries</u> due to tax losses

Charge 4: <u>Promotes forms of uncontrollable organized crimes against U.S. Citizens</u>

Charge 5: <u>Results in the violation of Article IV, Section IV of the U.S. Constitution,</u> where the federal government has a required duty and obligation to remove foreign invaders from U.S. soil and/or states harmed or threatened by them.

Charge 6: <u>Results in the violation of Article 1, Section 9, Clause 5 of the U.S. Constitution,</u> where "No Tax or Duty shall be laid on articles exported from any State."

Charge 7: <u>Results in the violation of the intent of the WTO by allowing import goods to be subjected to a reverse tariff.</u>

These are the charges; below we explain each and present the evidence to support our arguments.

2.2 Presenting the Details of the Case with Supporting Facts

We now proceed to present this case. We do so by detailing each charge and point to the locations in this book where the supporting evidence is detailed. It is the intent of this book to provide only substantial key evidence, we are limited in resources and do not wish to waste the readers time to detail all possible issues. Many of the charges use the same or similar evidence, so arguments are often related, but this should help the reader to understand the facts. It is hard to do justice to all the facts on trade deficit destructive effects available. We leave it up to congress to provide the actual justice America seeks.

The last chapter provides a signed petition by citizens who believe our trade deficit policy causes these destructive effects. We encourage the reader to sign the petition as well.

2.2.1 Charge 1: Trade Deficit Policy without any Limits Results in Unjustly Taking Money from U.S. Citizens

> **Brief description of Charge 1:** A U.S. trade deficit without limits causes the serious misuse of public funds. We claim the trade deficit literally takes money from each and every U.S. citizen through new taxes and entitlement losses. Such unjust activity would stop with a U.S. balanced trade policy or be reduced if the yearly trade deficit were at least limited.

More Detailed Description of Charge 1: The basic arguments for Charge 1 are that current U.S. trade deficit policy causes national debt primarily through multiple sources of U.S. tax revenue losses and forces excessive spending of government-funded unemployment programs. Evidence provided is from economic statistical studies (on how the trade deficit affects the national debt) and also includes our explanations. The qualitative evidence explains the tax losses in detail. However, quite simply, the U.S. government cannot collect taxes on foreign employees who replace U.S. workers. These replaced U.S. workers also end up in government-sponsored unemployment programs. This causes lost tax revenue which, combined with government unemployment program expenditures, creates increases to the national debt. U.S. citizens must pay for this increase. This is a form of unjustly taking money from citizens to support trade deficit products. Why, for example, should I have to partly pay for someone else's trade deficit purchase? We claim that all trade deficit products that are sold are in part subsidized by each and every U.S. citizen. U.S. citizens must incur the cost of trade deficit goods though tax losses. Since most of these goods are not in the interest of national security, we claim such costs are a serious misuse of public funds and is unjust. Only balanced trade can prevent this problem.

The public is now witnessing through the panic of Congress that public funds must be obtained to pay off the national debt which we have claimed is caused by trade deficit effects. The U.S. trade deficit steals jobs. Evidence shows that millions of job losses with 2.1 million of these lost due to high crimes of currency manipulation encouraged by the trade deficit effects. We show data of how combined job losses lead to separation of wealth by taking jobs and money from the poor and middle class and redistributing their wealth to both upper class Americans as well as foreigners. While many might argue that this is not robbing from the middle and lower class Americans, we know it to be unethical and perhaps at least a gray legal area. Americans have a right to keep good jobs and be protected from trade deficit criminal behavior of China's currency manipulation and other trade violations (i.e. counterfeiting of proprietary goods, patent and copyright infringements, etc.). All U.S. workers need representation rather than Congress only representing the wealthy. If balanced trade eliminates these effects, it is lawfully correct.

Evidence to Support Charge 1
The way we provide the supporting evidence in this book is by directing the reader to the appropriate chapter locations where the charges are substantiated. Similar to a court of law, each piece of evidence is provided as an Exhibit A, B, C, D, E or F. Since some exhibits cross multiple charges, it is appropriate to refer to them this way. This also allows the reader to review the evidence in as much detail as one would like. As well, it may help an actual court case to proceed if it comes to that.

The evidence for Charge 1 is both statistical and qualitative.

Exhibit A (and E, D-1) provides qualitative reasons for tax losses to support Charge 1. Such reasons help explain the problems associated with government revenue losses.

Table 2-1 Charge 1 - Qualitative Evidence

Exhibit	Description of Evidence	Chapter Section
A-1	MIT study on the trade deficit effects, tax losses due to lost jobs, outsourcing, offshoring.	3.1.2.1
A-2	Tax breaks for multinational corporations.	3.1.2.2
A-3	Examples of tax breaks for multinational corporation.	3.1.2.3
A-4	Deferral taxation of multinational corporations' tax shelter law.	3.1.2.4
E, D-1	Stealing jobs from lower and middle class Americans – Currency manipulation cost 2.1 of 3 million lost trade deficit jobs.	7.1, 6.1.1
A-5	Redistributing lower and middle class wealth to upper class Americans and foreigners.	8.1

Exhibit B (and A-5, E, D-1) provides the statistical verification that the trade deficit increases the national debt caused mainly by the tax revenue losses indicated in Exhibit A. Such reasons help statistically provide factual proof that such revenue losses exist.

Table 2-2 Charge 1 Statistical Evidence

Exhibit	Description of Evidence	Chapter, Section
B-1	An empirical analysis of the relationship between the budget deficit and the trade deficit, 1960-2003.	4.1.1
B-2	U.S. trade deficit creates budget deficit –NAFTA and China causality study, 1994-2007.	4.1.2
B-3	Correlation analysis –trade deficit and national debt (Study).	4.2.1
E	Trade deficit countries have higher unemployment. Higher unemployment is a key tax burden to U.S. revenues.	7.1
E, D-1	Stealing jobs from lower and middle class Americans – Currency manipulation cost 2.1 of 3 million lost trade deficit jobs.	7.1, 6.1.1
A-5	Redistributing lower and middle class wealth to upper class Americans and foreigners.	8.1

2.2.2 Charge 2: A Trade Deficit without Limits Policy Causes the Unjust use of Public Funds to Subsidize Importing Companies both Foreign and Domestic

Brief description of Charge 2: Companies are able to reduce the cost of products by manufacturing overseas. Such manufacturing practices cause tax losses. As well companies manufacturing overseas enjoy multiple tax breaks often termed tax loopholes for multinational corporations. U.S. taxpayers end up making up the difference, and this creates corporate subsidies. Such subsidies would stop with a U.S. balanced trade policy or be reduced if the yearly trade deficit were at least limited.

More Detailed Description of Charge 2: The basic arguments for Charge 2 are similar to Charge 1. Since current U.S. trade deficit policy causes national debt (verified by statistical studies) through multiple sources of U.S. tax revenue losses on imports, such imports are then effectively subsidized. Companies produce products not only with cheaper foreign untaxed labor, but have lobbied for tax loopholes, which enable excessive profits at the expense of U.S. citizens. U.S. citizens must pay for these lost revenues, which add to the national debt. Every tax loophole that benefits corporations is a cost to U.S. citizens. In addition to the losses in tax revenues are losses due to government unemployment programs. We devote much of an entire chapter on multinational tax loopholes for both foreign and domestic corporations. We note that each tax loophole that has been created over the last 20 years (since NAFTA and China entered into the U.S. marketplace) though the initiative of lobbyists and special interest corporate groups, has ended up penalizing U.S. citizens though increases to the national debt. Paying less corporate tax means someone has to pay for the lost revenues. This we reiterate is unjustly taking money from U.S. citizens who have to support the new tax breaks given to these multinational corporations. Why should U.S. citizens have to partially pay anything for the import business of U.S. companies? Companies are supposed to be self-supporting. We claim then that all trade deficit products sold are in part being subsidized by each and every citizen. U.S. citizens now must partially incur the cost of trade deficit goods and this cost then ends up as a subsidy. No such problem would exist in a U.S. balanced trade scenario. Thus, as trade is balanced, we provide evidence that such tax revenue losses would diminish and no national debt would be incurred from it.

Evidence to Support Charge 2
The evidence for Charge 2 is similar to that of Charge 1 and is statistical and qualitative.

Exhibit A also provides qualitative reasons for tax losses to support Charge 2. Such reasons help explain the problems associated with revenue losses.

Table 2-3 Charge 2 - Qualitative Evidence

Exhibit	Description of Evidence	Chapter Section
A-1	MIT study on the trade deficit effects, tax losses due to lost jobs, outsourcing, offshoring.	3.1.2.1
A-2	Tax breaks for multinational corporations.	3.1.2.2
A-3	Examples of tax breaks for multinational corporation.	3.1.2.3
A-4	Deferral taxation of multinational corporations' tax shelter law.	3.1.2.4
A-5	Redistributing lower and middle class wealth to upper class Americans and foreigners.	8.1

Exhibit B provides the statistical verification (that the trade deficit creates national debt) as explained by Exhibit A tax revenue losses. Such reasons help statistically provide factual proof that such revenue losses exist.

Table 2-4 Charge 2 Statistical Evidence

Exhibit	Description of Evidence	Chapter, Section
B-1	An empirical analysis of the relationship between the budget deficit and the trade deficit, 1960-2003.	4.1.1
B-2	U.S. trade deficit creates budget deficit –NAFTA and China causality study, 1994-2007.	4.1.2
B-3	Correlation analysis –trade deficit and national debt. (Study)	4.2.1
E	Trade deficit countries have higher unemployment. Higher unemployment is a key tax burden to U.S. revenues.	7.1
E, D-1	Stealing jobs from lower and middle class Americans – Currency manipulation cost 2.1 of 3 million lost trade deficit jobs.	7.1, 6.1.1
A-5	Redistributing lower and middle class wealth to upper class Americans and foreigners.	8.1

2.2.3 Charge 3: A Trade Deficit Policy without Limits Causes the Unjust use of Public Funds for the Purpose of Subsidizing the Transition of Domestic Business to Foreign Countries

Brief description of Charge 3: American companies find major tax advantages by transitioning their business to foreign countries like China. Each tax break is a government loss. Each loss adds to the U.S. debt causing more burdens to U.S. citizens who are now put in the position of paying and enabling the transition.

More Detailed Description of Charge 3: Trade deficit policy forces U.S. citizens to pay for the transition of U.S. businesses to foreign countries as they must support the unemployed who have lost their jobs in this transition. U.S. citizens would find it appalling if they realized they were in fact subsidizing such unethical activities through tax losses. However these activities are more than unethical; they create unjust use of public tax funds. This includes, but is not limited to, an increase in the national debt due to job outsourcing related to product off shoring, factory offshoring, tax loopholes in offshoring the business, and losses in U.S manufacturing. These tax losses mean that U.S. citizens are now being forced to pay a tax to partially support such business transitions. A limitless trade deficit policy makes favorable these business transition practices creating tax incentives. Every year, as businesses increase their global manufacturing base, they pay less and less taxes for offshoring their U.S. products. This again creates unfair use of public money for business activity purposes from citizens. As we mentioned before, businesses are supposed to be self-supporting and pay their fair share of taxes. However, these activities are effectively subsidized though government tax losses, passing the bill along to U.S. citizens who must then make up the difference and pay for additional nation debt incurred. These forced tax subsidies would stop with a U.S. balanced trade policy or be highly reduced if the yearly trade deficit was at least limited.

Evidence to Support Charge 3
The evidence for Charge 3 is similar to that of Charge 1 and 2 and is statistical and qualitative.

Exhibit A provides qualitative reasons for tax losses to support Charge 3. Such reasons help explain the problems associated with revenue losses.

Table 2-5 Charge 3 - Qualitative Evidence

Exhibit	Description of Evidence	Chapter Section
A-1	MIT study on the trade deficit effects, tax losses due to lost jobs, outsourcing, offshoring.	3.1.2.1
A-2	Tax breaks for multinational corporations.	3.1.2.2
A-3	Examples of tax breaks for multinational corporations.	3.1.2.3
A-4	Deferral taxation of multinational corporations' tax shelter law.	3.1.2.4

Exhibit B a verification of the tax revenue losses to support Charge 3. Such reasons help statistically provide factual proof that such revenue losses exist.

Table 2-6 Charge 3 Statistical Evidence

Exhibit	Description of Evidence	Chapter, Section
B-1	An empirical analysis of the relationship between the budget deficit and the trade deficit, 1960-2003.	4.1.1
B-2	U.S. trade deficit creates budget deficit –NAFTA and China causality study, 1994-2007.	4.1.2
B-3	Correlation analysis –trade deficit and national debt. (Study)	4.2.1
E	Trade deficit countries have higher unemployment. Higher unemployment is a key tax burden to U.S. revenues.	7.1

2.2.4 Charge 4: A Trade Deficit Policy without Limits Helps Promote Forms of Uncontrollable Organized Crimes Against U.S. Citizens

Brief description of Charge 4: Trade deficit policy without limits supports foreign organized crimes against U.S. businesses, which end up cheating U.S. citizens out of billions of dollars. These crimes include, but are not limited to, product counterfeiting, violations of U.S. intellectual property rights, currency manipulation, non-tariff trade barriers, and so forth. Such organized crimes would stop or be highly reduced with a U.S. balanced trade policy.

More Detailed Description of Charge 4: If trade were balanced, it would severely reduce organized trade deficit crimes. For example, adopting the 2006 Warren Buffett proposal of import certificates[65] would mean that any importer would have to purchase the certificate to sell their product in the U.S. This, of course, is only one scenario of possible methods to balance trade. However, under this scenario two things occur: 1) the importer would need another level of legal paper work to bring in their product, and 2) this is an added cost to a trade product, which, if it were a counterfeit product, would make it harder to enter into the U.S. The serious organized crime of currency manipulation would be 100% stopped as well. China's goal in currency manipulation is to create a Chinese trade surplus, which would not be allowed with a balanced trade policy.

We provide evidence that currency manipulation is responsible for the loss of about 2.1 million U.S. jobs. The U.S. government should seek retribution for these tax losses and the far-reaching business loss consequences that have occurred. Such retribution should most likely come from tariffs on all of China's imports, which could help pay off the national debt now partially created by these uncontrollable cheating practices by China. China also has a selective Value Added "tariff" Tax (VAT) of 17% charged to the importer (and not to domestic producers) while the U.S. has no equivalent import tax. This may not seem unjust, but since the U.S. has none, it adds to tax losses and, therefore, adds to the national debt revenue losses for which U.S. citizens must pay the difference. This tax is used by many countries and equates to a tariff.

---

[65] http://en.wikipedia.org/wiki/Import_Certificates

Evidence to Support Charges 4

The table below provides the location of evidence to support Charge 4. We provide numerous sources of evidence in the area of intentional trade violations by foreign countries, mainly China. This are highly organized crimes against the U.S., of manipulating currency, internet spying, creating unfair trade barriers, internet spying tactics, and intellectual property rights violations.

Table 2-7 Charge 4 - Evidence

Exhibit	Description of Evidence	Chapter, Section
D-1	China's currency manipulation cost 2.1 of 3 million lost trade deficit jobs.	**6.1.1**
D-2	Counterfeit goods – The largest underground industry in the world.	**6.2.1**
D-3	Patent, Copyright and Trademark Piracy, Testimony of Senator Gordon – China largest offender, Internet Spying	**6.2.2**
D-4	Japan's currency manipulation helps topple U.S. auto industry and Detroit jobs.	**6.3.1**
D-5-1	China's unmatched VAT tax – A comparative advantage.	**6.3.2**
D-5-2	China uses value added tax to keep out agricultural trade	**6.3.2**
D-6	General WTO violations.	**6.3.3**
D-7	China Owes the U.S. Trillions of Dollars in Trade Violations	**6.4**

2.2.5 Charge 5: A Trade Deficit Policy without Limits Results in the Violation of Article IV, Section IV of the U.S. Constitution

The federal government has a required duty and obligation to remove foreign invaders from U.S. soil and/or states harmed or threatened by them.

Brief description of Charge 5: Here the trade deficit is providing a path for foreign invasion through which foreigners now own a large portion of U.S. corporate businesses (21%) while the U.S. owns very little by comparison abroad (See Chapter 5, Figure 1). Such foreign invasion would be 100% stopped with a U.S. balanced trade policy or be reduced if the yearly trade deficit were at least limited.

More Detailed Description of Charge 5: At the end of 2011, the trade deficit was $8.5 trillion, which we have stated means that foreigners own that much more of us than we do of them. It is real debt that is paid off in their asset losses that is roughly split equally in their ownership of U.S. debt and their controlling interest in U.S. companies. As of January 2011 the estimates are:

- 21% of all revenue-bearing U.S. businesses
- 31% of our national debt

Foreign ownership also leads to serious tax revenue losses and is causing increases in U.S. unemployment. Foreign ownership is shown to have a high correlation to the trade deficit. This is because trade deficit dollars must be reinvested in the U.S. which enables such ownership. Our current projections are that 51% of all U.S. revenue-bearing businesses (and possibly our debt) will be foreign-owned in less than 25 years. Greater than 50% is considered as a controlling interest in the business world thus making this a foreign invasion. Balanced trade would stop this foreign invasion. Since we will not equally own foreign assets, we will end up losing control of our businesses and beholding to foreigners through our national debt making the U.S. more vulnerable to a foreign takeover (i.e. sizeable loss of our land, real-estate and businesses).

Evidence to Support Charge 5

The table below provides location of evidence to support Charge 5, that the trade deficit is providing a path for foreign invasion through which foreigners now own a large portion of U.S. corporate businesses without proper retribution which balanced trade would stop.

Table 2-8 Charge 5 – Evidence

Exhibit	Description of Evidence	Chapter, Section
C-1	Top American companies now foreign owned.	5.1
C-2	Foreign ownership of U.S. companies 51% by 2033 with skyrocketing U.S. unemployment projected.	5.2
C-3	Analysis of Internal Revenue Service data, Grant Thornton Report.	5.3

2.2.6 Charge 6: A Trade Deficit Policy without Limits Results in the Constitutional Violation of Article 1, Section 9, Clause 5

Brief description of Charge 6: As stated in our constitution, "No Tax or Duty shall be laid on articles exported from any State." Such tax violations would stop with a U.S. balanced trade policy or be reduced if the yearly trade deficit were at least limited.

More Detailed Description of Charge 6: The argument is then - U.S. tax payers are actually paying a "reverse tariff" tax on moving imported trade deficit goods from state to state through tax losses due to the trade deficit. In other words, U.S. citizens are paying an interstate tax since the import trade deficit goods have tax consequences that increase our National debt.

Evidence to Support Charges 6
The table below provides location of evidence to support Charge 6

Table 2-9 Charge 6 - Evidence

Exhibit	Description of Evidence	Chapter, Section
A-5	**Exhibit A-5** Reverse tariff trade deficit tax violates U.S. Constitutional law. Reference herein provides discussion with constitutional law professor.	3.2.1

2.2.7 Charge 7: A Trade deficit Policy without Limits Results in the Violation of the Intent of the World Trade Organization (WTO) Agreement

Brief description of Charge 7: The intent of the WTO agreement is to illuminate tariffs on most imports. Yet we will show that the trade deficit in fact creates a reverse tariff debt. Such reverse tariffs would stop with a U.S. balanced trade policy or be reduced if the yearly trade deficit were at least limited.

More Detailed Description of Charge 7: The agreement between our trading partners requires elimination of tariffs and quotas on most (if not all) goods and services traded between them. Our argument is similar to Charge 6. U.S. taxpayers are actually paying a "reverse tariff" on imported trade deficit goods through trade deficit tax losses. Since the trade deficit is partially funded by U.S. taxpayers, then this is a self-imposed tax on trade surplus of imports and is a reverse tariff debt that U.S. citizens are paying on deficit imports. Therefore, a trade deficit violates free trade policy itself!

Evidence to Support Charge 7
The table below provides location of evidence to support Charge 7.

Table 2-9 Charge 7 - Evidence

Exhibit	Description of Evidence	Chapter, Section
A-5	**Exhibit A-5** Reverse tariff trade deficit tax violates U.S. Constitutional law. Reference herein provides discussion with constitutional law professor.	3.2.1
A-6	Reverse tariff trade deficit tax violates the intent of the WTO agreement.	3.2.2
A-6	Explaining a reverse tariff trade deficit tax.	3.2.3

2.3 Closing Arguments

Ladies and gentlemen of the jury, you as the reader should review the evidence presented here. If you agree with all charges, you must find the trade deficit causes highly unjust and possibly illegal and unconstitutional activities and, therefore, it should be required by law to implement an alternate policy such as balanced trade that would prevent these problems. You then must act. It is the responsibility of each and every American to act by telling their representative to balance trade (see Chapter 9). It is then your Congressperson's sworn duty to uphold the law and the Constitution and seek to balance trade.

REASONS WHY THE TRADE DEFICIT CREATES NATIONAL DEBT

The relationship between the national debt and trade deficit has been studied over time, but not very well. These two are sometimes referred to by economists as the "twin deficits." Economists have had awkward theories on what effects one may have on the other. Today the data is fairly pronounced and can be verified statistically (see Chapter 4). Prior to such statistical proof, some economists in the past have wrongly believed that an increase in the national debt causes an increase in the trade deficit. We will not dwell on this. Their arguments have been proven wrong in economic studies (see next chapter) and their reasoning, highly inaccurate[66,67]. It has become clear that the trade deficit in actuality causes increases to national debt. When we assert this, we of course mean some portion of the national debt. The trade deficit is not responsible for the entire national debt.

It is important to state that any statistical verification should of course have qualitative reasoning as well. In this chapter we provide some strong qualitative reasons on why the trade deficit causes national debt. The idea of this chapter is to demonstrate some important reasons. Of course, more exist, and these should be considered when trying to make corrective actions. It is up to congress to do so.

---

[66] An Empirical Analysis of the Relationship Between the Budget Deficit and the Trade Deficit, Islam, Mazhar M.; Rahimian, Eric Journal of Academy of Business and Economics, February 1, 2005. Also see www.citizensforequaltrade.org for this article.

[67] U.S. Trade Deficit Creates Budget Deficit –NAFTA and China Causality Study, 1994-2007 *A. Feinberg, September 20, 2010,*
www.citizensforequaltrade.org/US%20Trade%20Def%20Causes%20National%20Debt%20-%20AFeinberg.pdf

It is important to note the U.S. twin peak milestone that occurred recently.

Remark 3.1: At the end of 2011, the trade deficit topped $8.5 trillion and coincidently, the national debt topped $15 trillion.

This milestone of course, should not be celebrated. It is a failure of macroeconomics and Congress to lack understanding on what a trade deficit can do to a country. The trade deficit is real debt. It is paid off silently in asset losses of real-estate sales, U.S. business sales, and the sale of treasuries to foreigners (now mostly China).

In a prior book by the author, we expressed the need for an "Office of Reliability and Quality Economics" which would be a bipartisan political economic solution to help congress people due proper problem solving. This is based on what industry uses to ensure that products are reliable over time. The industrial acceptance of the science of reliability and quality has made products over the globe improve and be dependable. We see that a lack of this science, which is not being adopted in economic practice, is partly to blame for our unreliable economy. Our country has no such bipartisan reliability economic solution (see Chapter 10 on the Economic Gap and Chapter 11, Appendix 1, on reliability economics).

The fact that the trade deficits create national debt in America is not an exception. Other countries have observed a similar relationship between these two[68]. It is no coincidence that countries like Greece and Spain are failing economically with high budget deficit crises. These countries also have a high trade deficit. As well, there are good examples of countries having a trade surplus such as Germany and China who do not have problematic budget deficits. On the other hand, we cannot make a full general statement that the reason for a country's budget crisis is primarily due to a country's trade deficit.

Nevertheless, it is imperative that any plan to reduce the U.S. national debt also includes a plan to balance trade. The mounting evidence here will show that it is an emergency.

Without balancing trade, taxpayers will continue to be penalized. That is all the tax losses gets billed to U.S. citizens. So companies that benefit in tax loopholes are actually subsidized by U.S. citizens from "trade deficit" goods. This makes it profitable to outsource jobs, and offshore factories (i.e. send manufacturing overseas); it encourages foreign cheating and robs the government of seriously needed revenues. The end results: U.S. citizens get a bill that helps pay companies to take away their jobs and opportunities. Foreigner companies also profit, specifically China, while their trade deficit profits

---

[68] Long-Run Linkage Between Budget Deficit And Trade Deficit In Lebanon: Results From The Uecm And Bounds Tests, Ali Salman Saleh, http://ideas.repec.org/a/ije/journl/v14y2006i1p29-48.html

enables the selling of America to foreigners who as we have explained, are gaining control of our country.

3.1 Trade Deficit Causes and Effects
The *causes* of the trade deficit should not be confused with the *effects*.

3.1.1 Trade Deficit Causes
Many economists have claimed that the cause of the trade deficit is due to lack of savings by citizens as a share of the GDP[69]:

> *The major changes in the U.S. trade deficit since 1970 can be traced to three primary sources: a long decline in saving as a share of GDP that began in the mid-1950s and accelerated in the 1980s, fluctuations in the business cycle, and relatively attractive investment opportunities in the United States in the 1990s.*

These early views (March 2000) are exceedingly naïve.

The primary causes of trade deficits are low wage earning countries (like China) selling to high wage earning countries (like the U.S.) and an aggressive Chinese government that will go to any length to dominate industries. (Note that oil imports are the other reason for the trade deficit). Then, of course, there is uncontrollable global economic greed which free traders naïvely ignore. These are effects, but also enhance and cause additional trade deficit. They include issues that we have mentioned such as product counterfeiting, violations of U.S. intellectual property rights, currency manipulation, and so forth.

Currency manipulation is the leading problem of the greed issue. Here the value of the U.S. dollar relative to the currency of our trading partners, specifically China (but also Japan and many other countries), can be critical in trade deficit creation. China has been under scrutiny as the biggest of the cheats for many years for undervaluing their currency, which keeps Chinese products artificially inexpensive, causing excessive imports and a reduction of U.S. exports. U.S. economists claim the price of the yuan is undervalued by *40 percent*. Presidents Bush and Obama have sought to alter Chinese policies through negotiations, but China promises have proven insincere.

3.1.2 Trade Deficit Effects – Tax Losses
In this chapter we focus on trade deficit tax losses. The below exhibits provide our evidence on reasons why the trade deficit causes national debt primarily due to tax losses.

---

[69] CBO, Causes and Consequence of the Trade Deficit, March 2000, www.cbo.gov/doc.cfm?index=1897&type=0

3.1.2.1 Exhibit A-1 – MIT Study, Job Losses Equates to Tax Losses
Every tax revenue loss is a burden to all U.S. citizens. Now the effect of the trade deficit is that it subtracts from demand for U.S. made goods and services. Consequently, a rising deficit slows economic recovery and job creation. Fewer jobs mean less tax revenue. These lost jobs, seemingly temporary, have continued yearly as U.S. manufacturing keeps declining.

The detailed effects of the trade deficit have been recently studied and are outlined below in a collaborative MIT study[70] funded partially by the National Science Foundation, Spanish Ministry of Science and Innovation, and from the community of Madrid. **We offer this study as Exhibit A-1, which we summarize as:**

Remark 3.2: *"…increased exposure of local labor markets to Chinese imports leads to higher un-employment, lower labor force participation, and reduced wages. The employment reduction is concentrated in manufacturing, and explains one third of the aggregate decline in U.S. manufacturing employment between 1990 and 2007. Wage declines occur in the broader local labor market, however, and are most pronounced outside of manufacturing. Growing import exposure spurs a substantial increase in transfer payments to individuals and households in the form of unemployment insurance benefits, disability benefits, income support payments, and in-kind medical benefits.*

Here we see a study that concluded what most Americans already know. The trade deficit creates serious job and business loss, leading to a loss of government revenues due to a decline in the labor force. Having a free trade policy that causes a large trade deficit actually tends to expand government by increasing the demand for social services, medical needs, and transfer payments (unemployment, welfare etc.) that are needed to mitigate these costs.

We showed in Chapter 1 in Remark 1.2 with basic economic math that just half of the trade deficit costs as many as 5,000,000 jobs. In Chapter 6 (Sec. 6.1.1), we show that about 2.1 million of these jobs is likely due to China's currency manipulation. Job losses may be seemingly temporary, yet they are occurring constantly enough due to outsourcing and offshoring of U.S. manufacturing and services. We cannot collect taxes from jobs that are outsourced to foreign employees. And many of U.S. jobless workers end up on U.S. Government subsidized programs including unemployment benefits and government sponsored retraining programs. An estimate of how much this might be costing the U.S. government is provided in Section 4.4. However, the unemployed

---

[70]D. Autor, D. Dorn, G. Hanson, The China Syndrome: Local Labor Market Effects of Import Competition in the United States http://econ-www.mit.edu/files/6613

also contribute very little to the U.S. economy and actually hurt the GDP growth. This cascades and accumulates yearly. It is a very hard to come up with a dollar value, but it is one the government should recognize in terms of trade deficit tax revenue losses creating more national debt. In terms of tax cut costs this has been quantified.

Job losses eventually cause large stimulus tax cut package. Many jobs were lost due to NAFTA in 1994 and continued after the entrance of China in October of 2001. It is of course hard to know the exact cause of the recession but in 2001, the famous Bush tax cuts started: they were passed in response to a recession occurring. These were the

- Economic Growth and Tax Relief Reconciliation Act of 2001
- Jobs and Growth Tax Relief Reconciliation Act of 2003

The Washington Post looked at the years from 2001 to 2011 and found[71]:

> **Remark 3.3**: *"...Tax cuts are estimated to have totaled $2.8 trillion.... Strictly speaking, the two big tax cuts during the Bush years are estimated to total about $1.5 trillion, but many continued into the early years of the Obama presidency, and in December he cut a deal with Republicans to extend them even more, which brings us to $2.8 trillion."*
>
> *"(... the cost of the Iraq and Afghanistan wars was $1.26 trillion through 2011 and the Medicare prescription drug program totaled $272 billion....)"*

A summary of the numerous stimulus packages provided by the Obama administration is provided at www.whitehouse.gov/issues/economy.

> **Remark 3.4:** *"...The $800 billion stimulus program Obama championed in 2009 turned into a political albatross for Democrats, with many voters feeling (mistakenly) that it drained the Treasury while doing nothing for the economy....Yet Obama has now negotiated an even bigger stimulus package. The price tag for the tax deal is about $900 billion over two years, which means money that would have been collected by the government will instead go into consumers' pockets, to spend as they see fit..."* [72].
>
> *"...President Obama has challenged Congress to immediately pass the American Jobs Act of 2011 – a $447 billion jobs package, including payroll tax cuts and tax credits to encourage hiring..."* [73]

---

[71] http://www.washingtonpost.com/blogs/fact-checker/post/revisiting-the-cost-of-the-bush-tax-cuts/2011/05/09/AFxTFtbG_blog.html

[72] http://caps.fool.com/blogs/900-billion-stimulus-for/488882

[73] http://www.cchgroup.com/webapp/wcs/stores/servlet/content_federal-tax-legislation_default

Indeed recently leading economists M.D. Chinn and J.A. Frieded explain the key issues behind the Bush tax cuts that were funded with massive foreign borrowing that fed our national debt crisis.[74] The need for tax cuts to spur job growth has a lot to do with U.S. manufacturing losses and their related job losses in the U.S. The controversy over the effectiveness of the Bush tax cuts is well documented[75]. The bottom line to our point in this chapter is that, all these government programs adds to the national debt.

Finally, we discussed the fact U.S. corporations are increasingly foreign owned. Our estimate in Chapter 5, as of January 2011, is 21% of U.S. businesses are foreign owned, but employ just 3.7% of U.S. citizens, showing how foreigners ownership costs U.S. jobs. Such ownership, (see Chapter 5), is enabled by trade deficit dollars transferred to foreigners, who buy U.S. businesses and cut jobs and result in lost taxes.

3.1.2.2 Exhibit A-2 – Tax breaks for multinational corporations

Every tax break for a multinational corporation is likely a burden for U.S. citizens as its end effect is to increase the national debt.

> ***Remark 3.5:*** *"In 2010, S&P 500 issues paid more income tax to foreign countries than to Washington," notes S&P's Silverblatt. "Only 46.4% of all income taxes paid by U.S. companies went to Washington in 2010 versus 53.6% paid abroad. Apparently, jobs weren't the only major export in 2010."[76]*

Corporate tax revenues have been on the decline. The below figure[77] provides an indication of the percent revenues collected from the corporate sector compared to individuals.

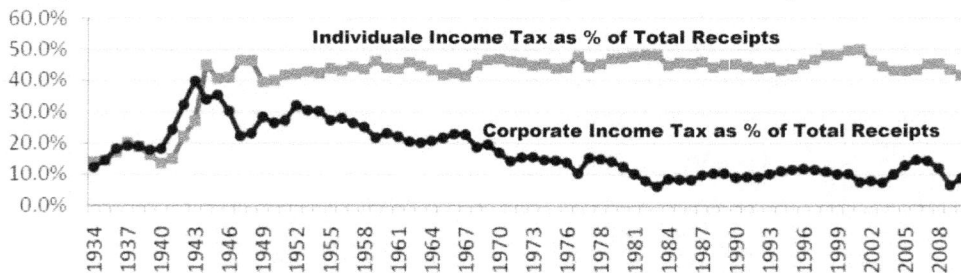

Figure 3-1 Decline of corporate taxes due in part to loopholes and lobbyist efforts

Today, 90% of government revenue is money coming from individuals with corpora-

---

[74] M.D. Chinn ,J.A. Frieded, Lost Decades: The Making of America's Debt Crisis and the Long Recovery.

[75] http://en.wikipedia.org/wiki/Bush_tax_cuts

[76] www.prnewswire.com/news-releases/foreign-sales-by-us-companies-tick-down-in-2010-463-of-all-sales-were-derived-outside-of-the-states-125804878.html, see full report at www.standardandpoors.com/indices/index-research/en/us

[77] www.policymattersohio.org/pdf/IssueBriefCorporateTaxation2011.pdf

tions paying well under 10% of all revenues collected (see Table 8-2)! Corporations lobby for tax breaks and their continued effort puts a higher tax burden on individuals. This is true of multinational corporations as well.

The following article appeared on the website Citizens for Tax Justice that explains the tax loss due to multinational corporations in the U.S. **We offer this article (which helps explain Remark 3.5 and Figure 3-1) as Exhibit A-2.**

Published by Citizens for Tax Justice (CTJ)[78]
Tax breaks for multinational corporations
By Robert S. McIntyre

Multinational corporations, whether American- or foreign-owned, are supposed to pay taxes on the profits they earn in the United States. In addition, American companies and individuals aren't supposed to gain tax advantages from moving their operations or investments to low-tax offshore "tax havens." But our tax laws often fail miserably to achieve these goals.

For example, IRS data show that foreign-owned corporations doing business here typically pay far less in U.S. income taxes than do purely American firms with comparable sales and assets.

1996-2002 Cost	
Corporate	$78 billion
Individual	$17 billion
Total	$95 billion

The same loopholes that foreign companies use are also utilized by U.S.-owned multinationals, and even provide incentives for American companies to move plants and jobs overseas.

The problems in our taxation of multinational companies stem mainly from the complicated, often unworkable approach we use to try to determine how much of a corporation's worldwide earnings relate to its U.S. activities, and therefore are subject to U.S. tax. In essence, the IRS must try to scrutinize every movement of goods and services between a multinational company's domestic and foreign operations, and then attempt to assure that a fair, "arm's length" "transfer price" was assigned (on paper) to each real or notional transaction. But companies have a

---

[78] Article reproduced - Courtesy of CTJ - The Hidden Entitlements - article on Tax breaks for multinational corporations. (Published here with permission from CTJ) www.ctj.org/hid_ent/part-2/part2-3.htm, other references include, www.ctj.org/pdf/corpwelf.pdf, www.ctj.org/html/corp0603.htm

huge incentive to pretend that their American operations pay too much or charge too little to their foreign operations for goods and services (for tax purposes only), thereby minimizing their U.S. taxable income. In other words, companies try to set their "transfer prices" to shift income away from the United States and shift deductible expenses into the United States. A May 1992 Congressional Budget Office report found that "increasingly aggressive transfer pricing by . . . multinational corporations" may be one source of the shortfall in corporate tax payments in recent years compared to what was predicted after the 1986 corporate tax reforms. Variants on the transfer-pricing problem--such as ill-advised "source" rules and statutory misallocations of certain kinds of expenses--expand the tax avoidance opportunities.

• *Let's say a big American company has $10 billion in total sales--half in the U.S. and half in Germany--and $8 billion in total expenses--again half and half (in reality). With $1 billion in actual U.S. profits and a 35% tax rate, the company ought to pay $350 million in U.S. income taxes. But suppose that for U.S. tax purposes, the company is able to treat 5/8th of its expenses--or $5 billion--as U.S.-related. If you do the arithmetic, you'll see that leaves it with zero U.S. taxable profit. Although our tax system has rules to mitigate this kind of abuse, companies still have plenty of room to maneuver.*

• *Here's a real-world example: In its 1987 annual report to its stockholders, IBM said that a third of its worldwide profits were earned by its U.S. operations. But on its federal tax return, IBM treated so much of its R&D expenses as U.S.-related that it reported almost no U.S. earnings--despite $25 billion in U.S. sales that year. As a result, IBM's federal income taxes for 1987 were virtually wiped out.*

• *Recently, Intel Corp. won a case in the Tax Court letting it treat millions of dollars in profits from selling U.S.-made computer chips as Japanese income for U.S. tax purposes--and therefore exempt from U.S. tax--even though a tax treaty between the U.S. and Japan requires Japan to treat the profits as American--and therefore exempt from Japanese tax! As too often happens, the profits thus became "nowhere income"--not taxable anywhere.*

• *Another of the classic tax avoidance games that multinational companies play is illustrated by a tax break that goes to the many drug companies and electronics firms that have set up subsidiaries in Puerto Rico. They assign "ownership" of their most valuable assets--patents, trade secrets and the like--to their Puerto Rican operations, and then argue that a very large share of their total profits is therefore "earned" in Puerto Rico and therefore eligible for the tax break. Reforms in 1986 tried to scale back this tax dodge, but it still costs more than $3 billion annually. Although encouraging jobs in Puerto Rico might be a nice idea(although perhaps not at the expense of mainland employment), it has been es-*

timated that many of the Puerto Rican jobs cost the Treasury upwards of $70,000 a year each because the tax break is so abused.

The official list of tax expenditures in the international area—totaling $95 billion over the next seven years--focuses on congressionally-enacted loopholes in the current "transfer pricing" approach. Thus, the list includes items such as indefinite "deferral" of tax on the profits of controlled foreign subsidiaries, misallocations of interest and research expenses, "source" rules that treat certain kinds of U.S. profits as foreign, and the Puerto Rican "possessions tax credit."[7]

Fixing these problems in the current system would be a good idea. But even better would be to replace the current, complex "transfer pricing" rules with a much simpler formula approach that taxes international profits based on the share of a company's worldwide sales, assets and payroll in the United States. Exactly how much revenue could be gained by this kind of comprehensive international tax reform is unclear, but some estimates are on the order of $15-20 billion annually.

Not listed in the official tax expenditure budget, but a major tax break nonetheless is the tax exemption for interest earned in the United States by foreigners. Such interest (on loans to American companies and the U.S. government) was exempted from U.S. tax under the Reagan administration in 1984. At the insistence of the proponents of the change, this interest income is not reported to foreigners' home governments, and as a result, tax evasion is said to be the norm. As a result, the United States has become a major international tax haven. There is evidence that not only foreign tax cheats, but also Americans posing as foreigners have been taking advantage of this loophole. Reinstating the tax has been proposed, with a waiver of the tax if a foreign lender supplies the information necessary to report the interest income to the foreign home government.

President Clinton pledged major international tax reforms in his 1992 campaign, but Congress rejected even the rather timid changes he proposed in 1993.The President's 1997 budget proposes $6.3 billion in international tax reforms over the 1997-2002 period, while congressional tax plans call for about a quarter that much. In addition, both sides want to scale back the $3 billion a year tax break for corporations in Puerto Rico by about half a billion dollars a year.

3.1.2.3 Exhibit A-3 Examples of Tax Breaks for Multinational Corporations

Below are articles where large multinational corporations that have lobbied for and received major tax breaks. We reiterate that every major tax break given to corporations then becomes a burden on U.S. citizens who have to make up for the lost government revenue, which adds to the national debt. In addition, each tax break eventually reduces the size of the middle class in America due to its impact on separation of wealth. Although this is a long-winded argument, it is clear that corporations who lobby for and receive tax breaks seek to avoid paying their fair share of our badly needed government revenue.

Exhibit A-3 Examples

March 2011 Published at Money.MSN.COM [79]: *"GE's corporate tax bill: Zero! The company didn't pay any US taxes in 2010. In fact, it got a tax benefit of $3.2 billion. The company has beaten Uncle Sam. It paid no U.S. taxes for 2010, <u>The New York Times reported</u>. In fact, it received a tax benefit of $3.2 billion…*

It's not that GE can claim poverty. The company made $14.2 billion in profits last year, including $5.1 billion from U.S. operations….How did GE do it? Through what the Times describes as "innovative accounting" and <u>fierce lobbying</u>, GE has been cutting its tax bill for years. <u>In a stroke of genius, it hired a former Treasury official to lead its tax department and filled its team with former IRS employees and Congressional tax specialists…</u>The top corporate tax rate is supposed to be 35% -- one of the highest in the world. But few companies actually pay that rate, since there <u>are myriad loopholes</u> and other ways to get breaks. Now, the Times reports, only 6.6% of Uncle Sam's tax revenue comes from corporations (down from 30% in the 1950s)….It's no coincidence that President Barack Obama installed GE's chief executive as the head of his new Council on Jobs and Competitiveness. One key subject the council is expected to address is taxes…"

Here we have the head of GE, CEO, Jeffrey Immelt, considered by many as Barack Obama's favorite businessman making a mockery of our system of government and dares to serve as the head of the president's Council on Jobs and Competitiveness. The consequences of GE's action is an increase in this company's profiteering and CEO entitlements while letting U.S. citizens now have to foot more of the national debt bill fill from the gaping financial hole that he creates not only for GE but the precedent he set for every corporation that benefits from GE's tax breaks he lobbied for on behalf of corporate America. Meanwhile honest taxpaying citizens are left with eventual losses of entitlements (like retiring at age 65, reduction in medical benefits, social security payment reductions, and increases in our tax bills, etc.). Americans are certainly asking the question, "Why should I have to sacrifice to pay off the national debt when corporate America companies like GE are not paying ANY taxes, and the wealthy are on average

---

[79] By <u>Kim Peterson</u> on Fri, Mar 25, 2011, http://money.msn.com/top-stocks/post.aspx?post=d715c70d-f0d0-4474-8223-2949588e90f6

paying only 17 to 23% income taxes[80] (see Table 8-1) indicating they are not paying their fare share either. The following article appeared in the Daily Beast regarding corporate tax breaks.

> **Remark 3.6:** *March 2011 Published in the Dailybeast.com* March 28th, 2010[81]: *"...Last year, Google reduced its tax burden by <u>$3.1 billion</u> by altering its tax practices. Boeing hasn't paid any federal corporate income taxes in the <u>last three years</u>, despite earning $10 billion in domestic pre-tax profit. Pharmaceutical companies <u>Pfizer, Eli Lilly, and Forest Laboratories</u> habitually avoid paying U.S. income taxes by recording profits in a country a world away from where the sales occur.... A study released in 2008 by the Government Accountability Office concluded that 57 percent of U.S.* companies doing business in the country paid *"<u>no federal income taxes</u> for at least one year between 1998 and 2005."...*

3.1.2.4 Exhibit A-4 Deferral Taxation for Multinational Corporations

Here again we remind the reader that tax breaks for a multinational corporation is a bill for U.S. citizens. We now present Exhibit A-3 with information describing deferred taxation which hurts circulation of money flow, jobs, and increase the national debt.

> **Remark 3.7:** (August 2011) ...In an analyst report in May, JPMorgan Chase estimated that 519 American multinational corporations had $1.375 trillion outside the United States due to the deferred tax breaks law...Tax policy is driving much of this trend. For multinational corporations, cash earned abroad cannot easily be remitted to the United States. If it is paid back to the United States, it is subject to a dividend tax that can rise to as much as 35 percent[82].

The following exhibit was published by the Citizens for Tax Justice in 2009 on this subject. Nothing has been done about the complaint as we see from the above remark.

> <u>*Published by Citizens for Tax Justice*</u> [83]
> *By Robert S. McIntyre, July 2009*
> **Multinational Corporate Tax Abuses, and Proposed Solutions: Summary of Comments by Robert S. McIntyre, Citizens for Tax Justice, at Capitol Hill Briefing on July 24, 2009**

---

[80] See – The Truth of the Modern Recession, A.A. Feinberg, Chapter 4. www.amazon.com/Truth-Modern-Recession-Reliable-Solutions/dp/0615315291

[81] www.thedailybeast.com/blogs-and-stories/2011-03-28/biggest-corporate-tax-cheats-from-general-electric-to-google-to-news-corp/

[82] http://dealbook.nytimes.com/2011/08/16/tax-policy-change-would-bring-cash-piles-abroad-back-home/

[83] Article reproduced - Courtesy of CTJ www.ctj.org/pdf/summaryremarksoffshorecorpabuses.pdf (published here with the permission from ctj.

Right now, big multinational corporations are making a mockery of our corporate income tax by manipulating our international tax rules. The root cause of this problem is that the U.S. does not tax corporations on the profits they earn abroad, at least not until they bring those profits back to the U.S.

Repeal of "deferral" would vastly simplify the taxation of multinational corporations and curb a wide array of abuses. The consequences of deferral are terrible.

First, in some cases, we are actually paying corporations to move plants and jobs abroad. Second, we are also paying corporations when they make their business appear to take place abroad, even if they don't actually move plants and jobs abroad. By using investment and transactions that only exist on paper (meaning no products or people actually leave the U.S.) they shift their profits (on paper) to countries that don't tax them. As a result, a big chunk of profits earned in the U.S. go completely untaxed.

A recent GAO report found that 83 of the 100 largest publicly traded U.S. Corporations reported having subsidiaries in these countries that don't tax corporate profits. The giant drug company Abbott Laboratories reported 36 such tax-haven subsidiaries. ExxonMobil has 32. The banking giant Citigroup has 427! A recent report from the Congressional Research Services found that corporations' shifting profits offshore costs the U.S. Treasury as much as $60 billion a year — lost revenues that have to be made up by average American taxpayers.

Conservatives often complain that the U.S. has a high corporate tax rate compared to other countries, but the effective tax rate is far lower because of these practices and other loopholes in our tax system.

As a result, U.S. corporate income taxes plummeted from almost a third of all non-Social-Security federal tax revenues in the 1960s to only a sixth of total taxes during the 2 George W. Bush administrations. U.S. corporate income taxes used to be among the highest in the world as a share of the economy. But now they rank near the bottom among all developed countries.

Although President Obama implied during his campaign that he might repeal deferral, he backed away once he took office. But the President does have some useful proposals to protect the U.S. corporate tax base by curbing some of the corporate tax abuses that have helped lead to this sharp decline in corporate tax payments. He would limit U.S. tax deductions for the costs of earning overseas profits. If corporations get to defer the U.S. taxes on profits they earn abroad, then surely they should also defer taking deductions for expenses related to that off-shore income. Our current rules actually provide companies with a negative tax rate on their foreign earnings!

The President also would narrow an egregious loophole that makes it far too easy for companies to artificially shift U.S. profits to tax havens. The President accurately called this "a loophole that lets subsidiaries of some of our largest companies tell the IRS that they're paying taxes abroad, tell foreign governments that they're paying taxes elsewhere— and avoid paying taxes anywhere."

The President proposals are not particularly harsh. If enacted, they would increase corporate tax receipts by only 5 percent. But they would be a step in the right direction toward leveling the playing field between U.S. and foreign investments and curbing egregious corporate tax sheltering.

On a follow up note, 2 years later we now see of course that corporations want more as they now are lobbying for tax breaks to bring this deferred foreign cash back.

Remark 3.8: *June 19, 2011, <u>Companies Push for Tax Break on Foreign Cash</u>[84]*
*Apple has $12 billion waiting offshore, Google has $17 billion and Microsoft, $29 billion....Under the proposal, known as a repatriation holiday, the federal income tax owed on such profits returned to the United States would fall to **5.25 percent** for one year, from 35 percent.*

Here we see the nature of hardships this greed will cost U.S. citizens[85]. Corporations somehow feel that only U.S. citizens are obligated to pay taxes for our national debt. They refuse to take responsibility for their fair share and push for more and more separation of wealth under the auspicious promise that they will use that money to create jobs – while the money will really be used to invest in factories in China! This will continue as long as the U.S. continues down its destructive trade deficit path.

3.2 Trade Deficit Tax – Reverse Tariff Violates Constitutional Law and the Intent of the WTO Agreement

In the appendix of this chapter, we describe in more detail the concept of a reverse tariff tax. One can also think of it as just a trade deficit tax due to the fact that the trade deficit causes national debt..

---

[84] http://www.nytimes.com/2011/06/20/business/20tax.html?ref=todayspaper&pagewanted=all#
[85] http://www.futureofcapitalism.com/2011/06/nyt-on-repatriation-tax-holiday

3.2.1 Exhibit A-5 Reverse Tariff Trade Deficit Tax Violates Constitutional Law

We have identified and verified with lawyer, Wesley Oliver, Professor of Constitutional law at Widener University, in March 2010 a violation of tax on interstate commerce. This constitutional law states (Article 1, Section 9, Clause 5): "No Tax or Duty shall be laid on articles exported from any State." The argument is then; U.S. tax payers are actually paying a "reverse tariff trade deficit" tax on moving imported trade deficit goods from state to state. In other words, U.S. citizens are paying an interstate tax since the import trade deficit goods have tax consequences that increase our national debt. Therefore, it is a violation of this constitutional law that tax payers are subsidizing the trade deficit on imported deficit goods that are moved from state to state across America. Therefore, only equal trade will not violate this law. We statistically validate in the next chapter that balanced trade would not increase national debt so that trade deficit reverse tax would not be incurred.

3.2.2 Exhibit A-6 Reverse Tariff Trade Deficit Tax Violates the WTO Agreement

The agreement between our trading partners requires elimination of tariffs and quotas on most (if not all) goods and services traded between them. However, this is not the case since U.S. taxpayers do pay a tariff, a "Reverse Tariff" on imported trade deficit goods. Therefore, any trade deficit violates free trade WTO policy! We know (see next Chapter) that if the trade deficit went to zero, the tax consequences (i.e. reverse tariff) would also end. This indicates that equal (i.e., balanced trade) would in fact be an excellent resolution to the trade deficit tax loss problems.

Appendix

3.2.3 Exhibit A-7 - Explaining a Reverse Tariff Trade Deficit Tax

Here we offer the explanation of the Reverse Tariff Debt as a formal exhibit. The following article published in *Economy in Crisis* explains the issues.

Reverse Tariff - Economic Crisis Due to Free Trade's Flaw
Published in Economy in Crisis, By Dr. Alec Feinberg on September 20, 2010

What is a reverse tariff? Like a tariff[86], a reverse tariff is a tax on imports (essentially a trade deficit reverse tax). However, a reverse tariff is defined here as a tax on imports paid on trade deficit goods and/or services, by the importing country's citizens due to trade deficit tax losses that occur. This presents an economic flaw of free trade. Therefore there are two key differences. The first is that instead of the importer paying the tax, the importing country pays the tax through tax losses.

---

[86] http://en.wikipedia.org/wiki/Tariff

The second key difference is that the tax losses are created by a trade deficit. Therefore, it is solely a tax only on trade deficit goods and services, since it is the trade deficit that causes the tax losses. These tax losses are real and effectively add to a country's national debt making it a debt that every citizen owes and must pay. Therefore, if you live in the United States which has massive trade deficits, it can and does cause economic hardship. To understand this we first need to comprehend why there are trade deficit tax losses. How do these come about?

There are both quantitative and qualitative reasons for tax losses. We will discuss the simpler qualitative reasons and provide the interested reader with reference to the quantitative ones. Here are basic examples of qualitative reasons for tax losses.

- Imports create decreases in federal tax revenues for various reasons, such as products made by non U.S. citizens who do not pay federal tax compared to products or services that would have created tax revenues if the products were not imported. Thus as U.S. made goods are replaced with foreign imports, so too are U.S. jobs and lost taxed wages in addition to unemployment benefits. Seemingly temporary, yet U.S. displaced workers occur frequently enough that the U.S. taxes burden is yearly.

- The U.S. trade deficit, now over $8.5 trillion (as of the end of 2011) since 1971[87], provides extra dollars to foreigners who can reinvest and buy treasuries and American businesses[88]. IRS data shows that foreign-owned corporations doing business here typically pay far less in U.S. income taxes than do purely American firms with comparable sales and assets. This is because it is hard to determine how much of a corporation's worldwide earnings relate to its U.S. activities and therefore are subject to U.S. taxes. There are many other tax issues that create serious tax problems[89] (see also 3.1.2). One key issue is that foreigner ownership produced few U.S. jobs ~3.7 percent (as of end of 2010 see Chapter 5)[90], while they own more than 21 percent (see Chapter 5) of all U.S. businesses.
- Many U.S. CEOs outsource jobs creating service trade deficit tax losses, these "imported services" decrease potential tax revenues of the company's workforce compared to non outsourcing and this also creates higher unemployment. Unemployment causes more lost tax dollars due to U.S. government subsidies until workers can recover.

---

[87] U.S. Census Bureau (2010),Trade Def. data, www.census.gov/foreign-trade/statistics/historical/gands.pdf,

[88] http://www.reuters.com/article/idUSN2744743020080827

[89] www.ctj.org/hid_ent/part-2/part2-3.htm, "Tax breaks for multinational corporations"

[90] http://www.nytimes.com/2009/10/18/business/18excerpt.html?_r=1

- U.S. companies' offshoring manufacturing find as much as a 15 percent tax reduction due to both tax loopholes and lower tax in other countries.

- Foreign profits from the trade deficit that are reinvested typically do not provide the tax revenue that U.S. citizen reinvestments may provide. For example, currently foreign reinvestments are considerable in U.S. government obligations for the U.S. national debt and now total about $4.5 trillion. This provides tax liability as the U.S. has to pay interest on this money to foreigners. On the other hand, U.S. citizens pay taxes on many of their reinvestments when owning U.S. business and equities. Foreigners who reinvest in buying U.S. business will also engage in job outsourcing once a U.S. business is taken over.

These are basic examples, but serve to help in understanding the reasons for tax losses from a trade deficit that creates the reverse tariff. Therefore, the trade deficit reverse tariffs mainly originate from job outsourcing, product outsourcing, and offshoring a country's factories and the ripple effect to our economy.

4

TRADE DEFICIT CREATES NATIONAL DEBT STATISTICAL STUDIES

Basic to free trade policy is the apparent fact that its trade deficit is responsible for a portion of the U.S. national debt due to trade deficit tax losses (that we have called a reverse tariff debt effect). Yet economists to date do not have any good estimate of how much of the national debt is caused by the trade deficit. We have provided in prior research a crude estimate.

> **Remark 4.1:** Our published estimate found that between 5 and 16% of the national debt is caused by loss of government revenues directly related to the trade deficit.[91]

It is really not our job to quantify this amount. It is the job of governmental macroeconomists.

It is their job because it is crucial in effecting government policy. Now more than ever as our government struggles to find a way to reduce the deficit, such estimates could help our Congress to see these facts and influence them to equalize trade as part of their plan to balance the budget.

Although no other current estimates are available that we know of, economists have statistically shown causality and the correlation between the two. In this chapter we present these statistics.

---

[91] The Truth of the Modern Recession, WE-Econmy Press, A.Feinberg, www.amazon.com/Truth-Modern-Recession-Reliable-Solutions/dp/0615315291

It is extremely important to provide this statistical evidence as the implications of the trade deficit causing national debt means that the average tax payer is subsidizing the trade deficit through increases in the national debt. This is paramount to a major problem in free trade and weighs heavily to the point of the unjust nature of the trade deficit question and to balancing our budget, job growth, and a healthy economy. Because of these facts, you might think that it would be a number one priority in macroeconomics to quantify this dollar amount. However, free trade macroeconomists for the most part skirt the issue. This is equivalent to turning a blind eye to a major unjust issue in our country, that of taking public money from the average tax payer to pay for the trade deficit and promote free trade policy. Free trade economists should not be taking this apathetic approach but should strive for the truth.

This chapter shows with statistics that yearly trade deficits are strongly tied to national debt increases. The results also indicate that when the trade deficit is reduced, its effect on the national debt is reduced. This seemingly obvious result indicates a very important fact that only balanced trade (i.e. equal trade) will not cause a trade deficit tax or reverse tariff (i.e. tax losses that adds to the U.S. national debt).

Below is a summary of the chapter's findings.

Chapter summary:

- In Section 4.2, we overview the statistical papers that demonstrate causality showing that yearly trade deficits from one year effect increase to the national debt the next year. This is called a time lag effect.

- In Section 4.3, we provide the details of how the trade deficit is correlated to the national debt with simple regression analysis. We suggest a crude model for determining how much of the national debt the trade deficit creates.

4.1 Introduction to the Statistics Causality Studies

It is fairly easy to show a correlation between the trade deficit and the national debt. We will do this in the next section. However, showing correlation does not demonstrate causality that the trade deficit causes increases to the national debt (or vice versa). Economists typically use a statistical method called a Granger-causality Wald test to show this. Trade Deficit (TD) is said to cause National Debt (ND), if the time series yearly lags of Trade Deficit can improve a forecast for variable National Debt (ND). For example, a lag means that the trade deficit in 1995 affects the national debt amount in 1996. This is a 1 year lag.

4.1.1 Exhibit B-1 – An Empirical Analysis of the Relationship Between the Budget Deficit and the Trade Deficit, 1960-2003

We offer as Exhibit B-1 a paper by Islam and Rahimian[92] that covered sequential years from 1960 to 2003. This paper found statistical evidence of the relationship between the U.S. government's budget deficit and the trade deficit by applying the Granger causality tests. Their results found

"...causality tests show a unidirectional causality between the trade deficit and the budget deficit... Contrary to the theory, our results show that the trade deficit "Granger Cause" the budget deficit."

Prior to this paper, most economists believed the opposite, that the budget deficit impacted the trade deficit, often termed the twin deficit theory. Here they thought an increased budget deficit was likely to put pressure on raising domestic interest rates, which in turn, would help raise the government capital needed. The value of the dollar would then appreciate along with the exchange rate, subsequently increasing imports and the trade deficit. There is a wealth of references in their paper for the interested reader on prior studies.

The contrary findings by these authors on the U.S. economy are not an exception. For example, A. S. Saleh, (2006)[93] studied the budget deficit and trade deficit in the developing country of Lebanon during the period from 1975 to 2003. His 2006 paper concluded,

"The Granger causality test shows that causality runs from trade deficit to budget deficit and the relationship is positive and statistically significant." He also concluded that, "any policy measures to reduce the trade deficit in Lebanon could well assist in reducing the Lebanese budget deficit."

The findings of Islam and Rahimian on the U.S. economy covered data up to 2003. We now have more data that can be studied. A study of later years from 1994 to 2007 is now published on the website, www.CitizensForEqualTrade.org and provided below. This study uses available government data that: 1) covers NAFTA (Dec. 1993) and China (Oct. 2000) entrance into the U.S. marketplace, and 2) was chosen as it is a relatively well-behaved data set. Below is the article presented in April 2011.

---

[92] Islam, M., and Rahimian, E. (2005). "An Empirical Analysis of the Relationship Between the Budget Deficit and the Trade Deficit", Journal of Academy of Business and Economics, 5-2, 1542

[93] Saleh, A.S. (2006), 'Long-Run Linkage Between Budget Deficit and Trade Deficit in Lebanon: Results from the UECM and Bounds Tests," Journal of Economics and Management, 13, no. 1: 29-48.

4.1.2 Exhibit B-2 – U.S. Trade Deficit Creates Budget Deficit –NAFTA and China Causality Study, 1994-2007[94]. (Note to the reader, this exhibit is not for the average reader as the statistics if somewhat specialized.)

By Dr. Alec Feinberg on September 20, 2010

1. Introduction

We report here statistical trends that the U.S. trade deficit causes a portion of its budget deficit using a Granger causality study. Many economists have debated whether the trade deficit causes national debt or vice versa. This study covers the sequential key years from 1994 through 2007. While this is a limited data period, we find strong trends to support the qualitative facts in Chapter 3. Such facts, while qualitative, are the basis for the statistics results. Thus the statistical finding for the small data set, are well supported. The subset years of available data are important as it 1) covers NAFTA (Dec. 1993) and China (Oct. 2000) entrance into the U.S. marketplace and 2) is relatively well behaved data set (i.e. with only 1 outlier). After 2007, data are confounded with outliers due to excessive U.S. budgetary increases from the U.S. recession. Additionally, before, 1994, the trade deficit was well under $100 billion per year and does not include NAFTA's influence. These outliers and yearly trade deficits are evident in looking at the labeled time series graph in Figure 1. The influence of NAFTA and China's entrance are particularly of concern, as their continual impact to the U.S. budget deficit needs to be understood where the U.S. trade deficit totaled over $8 trillion dollars at the end of 2010. Focusing on these select years provides pronounced statistical effects that are more discernable for determining the underlying causal relationship.

---

[94]www.citizensforequaltrade.org/US%20Trade%20Def%20Causes%20National%20Debt%20-%20AFeinberg.pdf

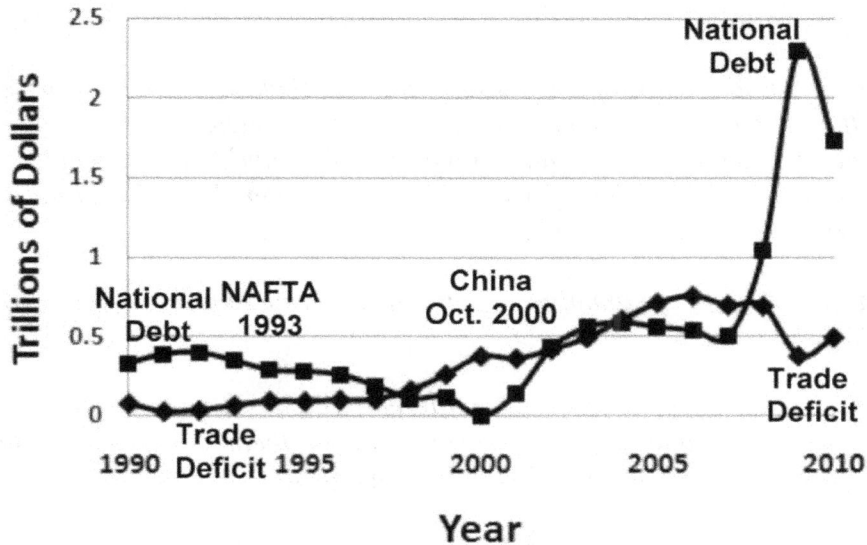

Figure 1 *Time series plot of the U.S. trade deficit and budget deficit 1990 to 2010, see Table 4-1*

2 Why is Causality Important

If the trade deficit causes national debt, then it means that consumers are essentially bearing the burden of trade deficit in the U.S. through eventual tax increase to help pay off the related budgetary increases. Taxpayers then somewhat subsidize both foreign and domestic companies who import products into the United States. The U.S. national debt is currently under scrutiny by Congress whose approach does not include a plan for trade deficit reduction. It is well advised from these results and other findings (see Islam and Rahimian, 2005), that such a plan should be developed.

3 Selected Review of Past Work

There are two types of consideration when looking at prior work, namely the statistical data provided here and the qualitative supportive facts. Such facts are in itself data of value. Without these, there is no reason to look statistically for supportive evidence. Here we have provided extensive argumentative facts in Chapter 3 detailing how influential the trade deficit has been on the national debt. The NAFTA and China data set is limited to a small but important set as discussed. Therefore, the statistical data becomes supportive for demonstrating causality budgetary trends due to NAFTA and China's influential U.S. impact. Such data will increase over time. But currently we need to address the econom-

ic concerns in a timely manner and are unable to wait for full collaborative evidence. However there is also prior statistical work that has been published.

There are a wealth of papers and findings that have cited theories and found different causal dependencies and non dependencies between the budget debt and trade deficit. Islam and Rahimian (2005), and Saleh (2006), provide excellent historical overviews for the interested reader. We will not bother to repeat these but only cite some of the key references.

In the Islam and Rahimian paper that covered sequential years from 1960 to 2003, they found

> "...causality tests show a unidirectional causality between the trade deficit and the budget deficit... Contrary to the theory, our results show that the trade deficit "Granger Cause" the budget deficit."

Table 4-1 Data set 1994-2007

Year	Trade Deficit (TD)	National Debt (ND)
1994	0.098	0.29
1995	0.096	0.28
1996	0.104	0.26
1997	0.108	0.19
1998	0.166	0.11
1999	0.265	0.12
2000*	0.38	0.03
2001	0.366	0.14
2002	0.422	0.43
2003	0.495	0.56
2004	0.61	0.59
2005	0.715	0.56
2006	0.76	0.54
2007	0.701	0.5
2008*	0.696	1.04
2009*	0.379	2.3
2010*	0.498	1.73

*Statistical Outlier Year well outside the 99.5% confidence band

4 Data Set of this Study

Data are examined from the U.S. Census Bureau. The data on the government budget deficits are from the White House office of Management and Budget, Fiscal Year, 2010 and is given from 1994 to 2010 in Table 4-1. From this data we select two subsets; Set 1, the years 1994 to 2007 and exclude the outlier year 2000, and Set 2 the same years but include the 2000 year outlier. Both sets exclude the outlier years from 2008 to 2010.

4.1 Relatively Stationary Parallel Data

Dividing the data set in half from 1994 to 2000, we see the influence of NAFTA, while from 2001 to 2007, we see the increase in TD due to China's impact now added to NAFTA's influence. This is important to realize as we do not expect the set to be stationary between the first and second half, but we do expect it to act in a parallel stationary manner between ND and TD. The table below is the observed results for the usable time between 1994 and 2007.

Table 4-2 *Stationary Data Analysis*

Statistic	TD	ND
Overall Mean (1994-2007)	0.3286	0.3776
Mean 1st Half (1994-2000)	0.1829	0.1739
Variance 1st Half	0.0099	0.0120
Mean 2nd half (2001-2007)	0.4743	0.5813
Variance 2nd Half	0.0245	0.0240

Here we note that both first half means are lower than the overall mean, while the second half means are greater than the overall mean. While this indicates that the data is rigorously non stationary, we see that the movements are in the same direction. Therefore, relative to each other the data are fairly stationary with both sets having similar variances for the first and second half. Furthermore, the fact that it is expected due to China's entrance at the end of 2000, correlates to this time period, and explains our observation. Under the assumption that the parallel movement are relatively stationary to each other for ND and TD and clearly expected, we proceed to look for influential causality trends.

4.2 Data Confidence and Control

There are 17 data points of which only 14 are used from 1994 to 2007. We limit the data to these years to provide some controls on the data variables. This represents a fairly small data set and confidence is greatly reduced with only 14 points. Nevertheless we show reasonable significance in the statistics for the cau-

sality results. The purpose in fact is to target the NAFTA and China years. As we mentioned before, it is important to be timely and not wait for more years to pass, in light of the qualitative facts in Chapter 3 and the warning signs we are seeing.

Furthermore, the data set chosen is well behaved when removing 2008, 2009, and 2010 which were highly irregular in government spending mostly due to the recession. Therefore as a control to the recession's impact, these years are best removed. Any further controls might be looked at as confounding and providing bias to the raw data. No further controls were used to study the underlying relationship.

5   Granger Causality Study

The test used here and by most economists is the Granger causality test. The theory of cointegration, was first introduced by Granger (1980) and then developed by Granger (1986,) and Engle and Granger (1987). The degree to which effects operate in each direction can be assessed by a Granger-causality Wald tests. Trade Deficit (TD) is said to Granger cause National Debt (ND), if the lags of TD can improve a forecast for variable ND.

Here we test the significance levels for the null hypothesis that the trade deficit does not Granger-cause the fiscal deficit and vice versa for 1 year lag using the data Set 1 (without year 2000) and Set 2 (with year 2000) in Table 4-1. In order to ascertain the results with 1 lag for Set 1, we chose to model it as a continual time series. This is done in order to see the level of the effect the year 2000 outlier has on the full Set 2 time series by comparing the two.

Table 4-2 *Granger Causality Wald Test Results at the 95% Confidence Level**

Data Set No.	Dependent Variable Y	Regressor X	Chi^2	Prob > Chi^2 (P)	N	Period	Year 2000 Excluded
1	ND	TD	3.381	0.066	1 2	1994-2007	YES
1	TD	ND	0.182	0.67	1 2	1994-2007	YES
2	ND	TD	2.4086	0.121	1 3	1994-2007	NO
2	TD	ND	0.1256	0.723	1 3	1994-2007	NO

* Result using Stata software – also see Appendix B

The Granger causality Wald test results are summarized in Table 4-2 and show reasonable level of significance regarding causality for both Sets 1 and 2 (full re-

sults are in Appendix B) despite the small data set. We note the effect the year 2000 outlier has on Set 1 with significance P-level of 0.066 compared to 0.121 for Set 2.

The Granger causality is observed below the ten percent level for TD acting on ND for Set 1 and is close to this level for Set 2. In Set 2 we then can justify and take the conservative approach and accept that there is a reasonable level of significance to warrant that causality does significantly exist. These results with and without outlier provide evidence of significant unidirectional causation that the trade deficit does Granger cause national debt, This is in agreement with Islam and Rahimian, (2005) which found similar results up to 2003.

Finally, two lag results were not statistically significant. In this case, the result showed good significance in the relationship between national debt and trade deficit, but no discernable causality.

Conclusion
Our results show a reasonable unidirectional causality running from the trade deficit to the budget deficit. No causality has been found from the budget deficit to the trade deficit.

This study provides statistical support and given the suggested qualitative factual reasons summarized in Chapter 3, it demonstrates serious concerns about America's Trade deficit influence on the U.S. national debt. We agree with the conclusion of the Saleh (2006) study that found similar results for his country and also suggested, "any policy measures to reduce the trade deficit in Lebanon could well assist in reducing the Lebanese budget deficit." We feel that this applies in particular to the U.S. trade policy.

References
Dewald, William G. (1983). "Federal Deficits and Real Interest Rates: Theory and Evidence", Economics Review, Federal Reserve Bank of Atlanta 48, no.1.: 20-29.

Dwyer, Gerald, P. (February 1986). "Inflation and Government Deficits", Economics Inquiry 20, no.3. July 1982: 315-329.

Engle, Robert F., Clive W. J. Granger (March 1987). "Co-integration and Error Correction: Representation, Estimation and Testing", Econometrica 55, no.2.: 251-276.

Evans, Paul (March 1985). "Do Large Deficits Produce High interest Rates?" American Economics Review 75, no.1: 68-87.

Feinberg, A (September 2010), "Reverse Tariff - Economic Crisis Due to Free Trade's Flaw", http://economyincrisis.org/content/reverse-tariff-economic-crisis-due-free-trades-flaw

Feinberg, A. (2009), The Truth of the Modern Recession, WE-Economy Press
http://www.amazon.com/Truth-Modern-Recession-Reliable-
Solutions/dp/0615315291
Fleming, J. M. (1962) "Domestic Financial Policies under Fixed and under Floating
Exchange Rates." International Monetary Fund Staff, Papers 10: 369-380.

Granger, C.W.J. (August 1986). "Development in the Study of Cointegrated Va-
riables", Oxford Bulletin of Economics and Statistics. 48,: 213-227.

Granger, C.W.J.. (1980). "Some Development in a Concept of Causality," Journal of
Economic Dynamics and Control. 2.: 329-352.

Hoelscher, Gregory P. (February 1986). "New Evidence on Deficits and Interest
Rates", Journal of Money, Credit and Banking 18, no.1.:1-17.

http://economyincrisis.org/content/reverse-tariff-economic-crisis-due-free-trades-
flaw
Hutchinson, Michael M. and Charles Pigott (1984). "Budget Deficits, Exchange
Rates and Current Account; Theory and U.S. Evidence", Economics Review, Federal
Reserve bank of San Francisco, 5-25.
Islam, M., and Rahimian, E. (2005). "An Empirical Analysis of the Relationship Be-
tween the Budget Deficit and the Trade Deficit", Journal of Academy of Business
and Economics, 5-2, 1542
McIntyre, R. (2003). "Tax Breaks for Multinational Corporations",
www.ctj.org/hid_ent/contents/content.htm#shelly
Mundell, R.A. (1963). "Capital Mobility and Stabilization Policy Under Fixed and
Flexible Exchange Rates." Canadian Journal of Economics and Political Science
29: 475-85.
Saleh, A.S. (2006), 'Long-Run Linkage Between Budget Deficit and Trade Deficit in
Lebanon: Results from the UECM and Bounds Tests," Journal of Economics and
Management, 13, no. 1: 29-48.
U.S. Census Bureau (2010),Trade Def. data, www.census.gov/foreign-
trade/statistics/historical/gands.pdf,
White House, Office of Management and Budget (2010),
http://www.whitehouse.gov/omb/budget/Historicals

Exhibit B-2 Article Appendix - Statistical Granger Software Results

Table B.1 Stata Software output

Vector Autoregression

Data Set 1: 1994-2007 with outlier year 2000 omitted

No. of Observations= 12, Log Likelihood=31.788, FPE=0.0000476, Det(Sigma_ml)=0.0000171

AIC = -4.298, HQIC = -4.388, SBIC=-4.0555

Equation	Parms	RMSE	R-Sq	Chi2	P>Chi2
td	3	0.05894	0.9566	264.7	0.0000
nd	3	0.09663	0.7917	45.6	0.0000

		Coef.	Std. Err.	z	P>|z|	95% Lower Conf. Interval	95% Upper Conf. Interval
td							
	td L1.	1.0326	0.10125	10.20	0.00	0.8341	1.231
	nd L1.	-0.0577	0.13515	-0.43	0.670	-0.3226	0.2072
	cons	0.0584	0.03142	1.86	0.063	-0.00319	0.1199
nd							
	td L1.	0.3070	0.16699	1.84	0.066	-0.02025	0.6343
	nd L1.	0.5520	0.2228	2.48	0.013	0.11519	0.98885
	cons	0.0618	0.0518	1.19	0.233	-0.3972	0.16342

.vargranger

Granger Causality Walt Test

Equation	Excluded	Chi2	Df	Prob > chi2
td	nd	0.18207	1	0.670
td	ALL	0.18207	1	0.670
nd	td	3.3808	1	0.066
nd	ALL	3.3808	1	0.066

Stata Software Output, Data Set 1: 1994-2007 with outlier year 2000 omitted is provided in Table B.1. The trade deficit is td, and the national debt is nd.

4.2 Correlation Analysis – Free Trade and National Debt

Here we provide a correlation analysis between the national debt and the trade deficit. We can just look at the raw data and see what it is telling us. One caveat is that there is a problem when doing this. This is because we showed in the last section that there is a one year time lag for the trade deficit to cause national debt changes. This means that what occurs on the trade deficit in one year lags, i.e., does not show up to affect the national debt to the next year. Therefore, the correlation equation is not perfectly valid. However, assessing correlation is really the first step in looking to show that there is a relationship. The degree of correlation is an indication of how well they are related. We have found that whether we put in a lag or not, the correlations do not turn out to be that mathematically different. The following is an excerpt from the book, the Truth of the Modern Recession.

4.2.1 Exhibit B-3: Correlation Analysis – Trade Deficit and National Debt
A. Feinberg, originally published in the book, The Truth of the Modern Recession

Here we use a simple mathematical correlation assessment that should be helpful as part of our reliability economic investigation. Correlations are sought all the time in many areas. For example in health, we know that being overweight is correlated to diabetes; smoking has been correlated to lung cancer and emphysema, and so forth.

In a similar manner, we suspect that the U.S. trade deficit may be linked to America's national debt due to related Trade Deficit Tax (TDT) losses.

Despite the complex nature in interpreting the data, mathematically we simply will look at the raw data. Results show below that a correlation exists of about 84% in select reasonable time periods between 1990 and 2008. First we mention that it is clear the two can be unrelated in certain time periods. For example, we know that the trade deficit in 1990 to about 1995 was minimal compared to the national debt (see Table 4-3). At this point in time where the trade deficit was just starting to accumulate, tax losses would be minimal. Similarly, one would anticipate a weaker correlation in 2008 and 2009, since the U.S. expenditures have been highly irregular due to the modern recession compared to the trade deficit which has dropped dramatically due to the recession.

To perform this simple assessment, we provide the trade deficit data (from the U.S. Census.gov website. This is listed in Table 4-3. Column 2 provides the trade deficit data in trillions of dollars. Columns 3 and 5 reflect the cumulative results and the running totals of each.

First we will look at the raw data in select years that make sense where we expect a correlation to occur. In order to identify the possibility of a mathematical correlation, logically certain years are able to reveal the underlying relation better than other periods in the historical data set. Then the select year assumptions are:

1) Select a reasonable sequential time period within the normal 20 year time frame of interest. We stated earlier that from 1990 to 1995, there was a minor trade deficit and there was little correlation.

Table 4-3 *National Debt and Trade Deficit Data (1990-2009)*[95]

Year	Annual Trade Deficit in Trillions $	Cumulative Trade Deficit in Trillions $	National Debt in Trillions $	Cumulative National Debt in Trillions $
1990	0.081	1.01[+]	0.33	3.21
1991	0.031	1.04	0.39	3.6
1992	0.039	1.08	0.4	4
1993	0.070	1.15	0.35	4.35
1994	0.098	1.25	0.29	4.64
1995	0.096	1.35	0.28	4.92
1996	0.104 M1	1.45	0.26	5.18
1997	0.108 M1	1.56	0.19	5.37
1998	0.166 M1	1.73	0.11	5.48
1999	0.265 M1	1.99	0.12	5.6
2000	0.380	2.37	0.03**	5.63
2001	0.366 M1	2.74	0.14	5.77
2002	0.422 M1	3.16	0.43	6.2
2003	0.495 M1	3.65	0.56	6.76
2004	0.610 M1	4.26	0.59	7.35
2005	0.715 M1	4.98	0.56	7.91
2006	0.760 M1	5.74	0.54	8.45
2007	0.701 M1	6.44	0.5	8.95
2008	0.696	7.14	1.04	9.99
2009	0.379	7.52	2.3	12.3
2010	0.498	8.02	1.73	14.02

We also noted that 2008 and 2009 were highly irregular in government spending. These years will be ignored in the correlation analysis.
2) We use values M1 in Table 4-3, a set of 11 years from 1996 -2007 to look for a correlation. We ignore an irregular point, the year 2000 (a statistical outlier).

---

[95] Trade Def. Ref. http://www.census.gov/foreign-trade/statistics/historical/gands.pdf,
National Debt Ref: www.whitehouse.gov/omb/budget/fy2010/assets/hist.pdf (may be revised)
** Outlier point - an irregular data point. [+]Accumulated trade deficit since 1971

Next we look at the raw data by performing a regression analysis of Col. 2 and Col. 4 shown in Figure 2. This provides an estimate of how well the national debt and trade deficit correlate. This is obtained from R^2 of 0.711. The square root of this values is the correlation coefficient of 0.84 (R-value), indicating an 84% correlation, in this select period from 1996 to 2007. Figure 2 also shows the 95% confidence bounds about the regression line. The P-value found of 0.001 (Figure 9.3) indicate a probability of 1 in a 1000 that the correlation is by chance. A "Durbin-Watson" statistic for Model 1 was 0.96. This large value (> 0.8) indicates an unlikely autocorrelation.

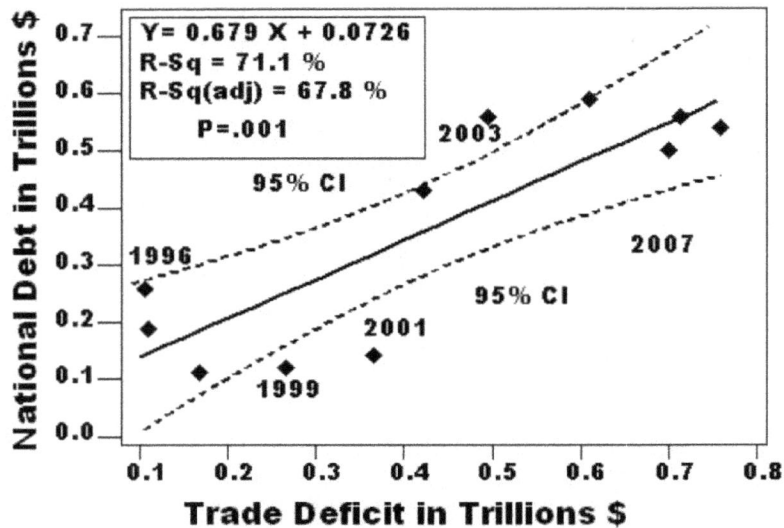

Figure 2 *Model 1 of the national debt versus the trade deficit, 1996 to 2007*

The actual dollar relationship is potentially challenging due to the time lag that we discussed earlier. We note the slope in Figure 2 is given by the X-Y re-lationship on the graph (i.e. Y=0.679X+.0726). First note the Y intercept (.0726) is relatively small compared to values in Column 3 from 1996-2007. This implies there would be little or no tax consequence to the national debt if the trade deficit were zero.

As we mentioned in Chapter 3 there are many reasons why this high cor-relation exists. One complex reason is foreigners reinvest trade deficit dollars in businesses and treasuries. While this can help GDP growth for new investment and tax revenue through businesses and new job creation, there are also lost rev-enues that can be greater. For example, foreign treasury investments mean that interest must be paid by the U.S. Government to foreigners and that cost revenue dollars. About 40% of $8 trillion is invested in treasuries equating to $3.2 trillion. As well, foreigner business investments have shown poor U.S. job creation (see

*Chapter 5), and manufacturing and associated jobs are typically outsourced. We see that free trade is not really free due to this **reverse tariff debt**!*

4.3 Estimated Displaced Trade Deficit Jobs Lost

While it is true that exports support jobs in the United States, it is equally true that imports displace them. The net effect of trade flows on employment is determined by changes in the trade balance

Remark 4.2: *"The High Price of "Free" Trade, November 17, 2003: Since the North American Free Trade Agreement (NAFTA) was signed in 1993, the rise in the U.S. trade deficit with Canada and Mexico through 2002 has caused the displacement of production that supported 879,280 U.S. jobs... Manufacturing industries were responsible for 78% of the net jobs lost under NAFTA, a total of 686,700 manufacturing jobs."[96]*

Remark 4.3: *An Economic Policy Institute study claims that the trade deficit with China cost more than 2.4 million U.S. jobs between 2001 and 2008[97]*

Remark 4.4: *"U.S. NAFTA Trade Deficit Surging Again Snapshot for November 5, 2003: The rise in the U.S. deficit with Canada and Mexico from 1993 to 2000 displaced production supported by 766,000 U.S. jobs. Most of those jobs would have been high-wage positions in manufacturing industries." [98]*

Remark 4.5: *Between NAFTA and China spanning 1993 and 2008 the total job outsourcing loss is at least 3.2 million.*

Remark 4.6: *Another way to provide a rough estimate on jobs lost relative to the trade deficit is as follows:*

First we find the GDP job productivity per worker on average over the last 5 years is as follows:
- *On average there were about 150 million workers[99] in the U.S. over this period*

---

[96]www.policyarchive.org/bitstream/handle/10207/8113/epi_bp147.pdf?sequence=1
[97] http://online.wsj.com/article/BT-CO-20100323-713114.html?mod=WSJ_latestheadlines
[98]/www.epi.org/economic_snapshots/entry/webfeatures_snapshots_archive_11052003/
[99] www.bls.gov/cps/cpsaat1.pdf

- *The U.S. GDP 5 year averaged is roughly $13.5 trillion*
- *This equates to about $90,000 of productivity per worker in GDP contribution*

The annual trade deficit average over the last 5 years is about $600 billion per year. We estimate that about 55% of this is due to Oil imports[100]. The other portion, 45% or $270 billion, is what we model as having the main impact on trade deficit job losses. The job lost estimate is then:

$270,000,000,000/$90,000=3 Million jobs lost due to the trade deficit

This is fairly close to the 3.2 million job estimate above.

4.4 How Much National Debt is caused by the Trade Deficit?

We have mentioned previously, estimating how much of the national debt is created from the trade deficit is a difficult estimate and should be one that government economists are required to figure out. We will provide some crude quick numbers to show that possibly as much as 10 to 30% of the trade deficit each year causes national debt. This currently equates to $60 billion or as high as $180 billion (where the trade deficit has been averaging about $600 billion in the years of our estimate).

Consider the period from 2001 to 2008. We will roughly estimate 3 contributing factors that add to the national debt from trade deficit tax losses. These are:
- Tax losses due to lost trade deficit jobs
- Compound tax losses due to interest on the national debt paid to foreigners
- Tax losses due to loopholes from multinational corporations

Tax losses due to Jobs lost

We have estimated 3.2 million jobs lost from our prior discussion. The EPI estimates that between lost taxes from layoffs and government unemployment programs, it has cost the U.S. government about $700 per week[101] for each unemployed worker. If we assume on average that an unemployed worker received a full year benefit, this equates to about $116 billion (=3.2 million x 52 weeks x $700/week) of lost government revenues.

Tax losses due to Interest Paid to Foreigners

The total national debt at the end of 2008 that was owned by foreigners was about $3 trillion (about 1/3 of the total) of which $1.45 trillion foreign debt occurred from

---

[100] www.dailymarkets.com/stock/2011/05/11/trade-deficit-up-on-oil-addicition/, Trade Deficit Up On Oil Addiction, Dirk Van Dijk, May 11, 2011
[101] www.epi.org/publications/entry/jobs_crisis_fact_sheet/

2001 through 2008. The interest on this averaged about 3.2%[102]. If we assume compound interest paid out over 8 years on this portion of the national debt this comes to about $117 billion paid to foreigners. The total is then $232 billion ($116 + $117 billion). The $232 billion equates to 5.3% of the $4.36 trillion national debt or about 4.9% of the total trade deficit in this period from 2001 to 2008 (total trade deficit and national debt were about equal then).

Tax losses due to Multinational Corporation Tax Loopholes
There is no easy way to estimate the amount of tax losses due to multinational corporation tax loopholes. We certainly see that in 1970, corporations paid about 20% of all IRS revenue collected and only paid about 10% now (see Figure 3-1) in 2008. We can possibly justify another 5% loss. This amount would double the tax losses that have occurred to about 10% of the trade deficit. Now add to this the lost revenues from illegal trade activities, currency manipulation, foreigners purchasing U.S. businesses creating lost taxes, etc. We might well justify this additional amount and more.

At the end of 2010, for example, using this 10% value, the trade deficit accumulated to $8 trillion and 10% of this is $800 billion lost revenues.

Other Statistical Estimates
As a final note in the appendix of Exhibit B-2, in Table B.1, the coefficient indicates that as high as 30.7% of the trade deficit may cause national debt. From our estimates this seems high. However, it is very concerning and government economists should be looking at this issue very seriously.

---

[102]http://money.cnn.com/2011/02/02/news/economy/interest_national_debt/index.htm

5

TRADE DEFICIT POLICY SUPPORTS FOREIGN INVASION - 51% OWNERSHIP BY 2033

Foreign ownership of U.S. companies is not just on the rise, but it is quickly closing in on a controlling interest in the United States. Many might ask, what happened to the country that Americans fought and died for? We blame the trade deficit for this. As a point of clarification for the reader, U.S. trade deficit foreign profits are in U.S. currency. So when a foreigner has X-amount of U.S. dollars from trading profits, that money has to eventually find its way back in reinvestment in America. As we have mentioned, the trade deficit passed the $8.5 trillion mark at the end of 2011 and those reinvested monies have helped enable foreign ownership. This is the concept of free trade. It shows how free trade economists do not understand the logical consequences of this policy. By December of 2011, foreigners owned $8.5 trillion (Exhibit B-3) more of us than we do of them. This is also true of foreign ownership of U.S. debt. As of January 2011 the estimates are now:

- 21% of all revenue-bearing U.S. businesses
- 31% of our national debt (about $3.2 trillion of $14 trillion national debt)[103, 104]

As we will discuss below, foreign ownership leads to serious tax revenue losses and is projected to skyrocket U.S. unemployment, currently occurring. To put the unem-

---

[103] www.treasury.gov/resource-center/data-chart-center/tic/Documents/mfh.txt
[104] www.usdebtclock.org/

ployment in perspective, the 21% ownership leads to just about 3.7%[105] U.S. employment. Multiply this number up by 5 and that would indicate that if foreigners owned 100% of U.S. businesses they would only employ 19% of U.S. citizens. This is another indication that the U.S. Government has no realistic grasp of the depth of our pending unemployment problem related to the U.S. trade deficit. The U.S. Trade deficit is mainly with China as the table below indicates. The full table is shown in Chapter 12 Table 12-1.

Table 5-1 U.S. Trade Deficit Information in Billions of Dollars[106]

| Year | Goods Only | | | | | China Percent of Total | U.S. Goods & Service Total Trade Deficit |
	China	Japan	Mexico*	Canada*	Others		
2011	-$296	-$63	-$66	-$36	-$99	53%	-$558
2010	-$273	-$60	-$68	-$28	-$71	55%	-$500

The large yearly trade deficit is a debt that is paid off in the selling of America's land, businesses and treasuries totaling in assets over the $8.5 trillion. We mentioned in Chapter 1 that this can be viewed as a foreign invasion. Here we will show that foreigners are projected to own 51% of all U.S. revenue-bearing businesses (and possibly our debt) in less than 25 years. If this occurs, unemployment is anticipated to skyrocket to possibly 36%. In corporate America, 51% ownership equates to a legal controlling interest. Since we are all shareholders in America, at what point do we ask the unthinkable question, ***"If foreigners own 51% of America, than do Americans still own and control their country?"*** If your answer is no, i.e. Americans will not be able to own or control their own country, then you must come to the inevitable conclusion that the country will essentially be owned and controlled by foreign governments. If this is the case, then we have underway a foreign invasion which is unconstitutional.

Here are some shocking examples of what is going on. Foreign ownership now includes some of the most famous American iconic companies. An example short list of foreign ownerships is provided in the first exhibit:

5.1 EXHIBIT C-1 Top American Companies Now Foreign Owned[107]

---

[105] A Lifeline Not Made in the U.S.A, M. Maynard, October 17, 2009, www.nytimes.com/2009/10/18/business/18excerpt.html
[106] http://www.census.gov/foreign-trade/balance/
[107] www.msnbc.msn.com/id/41536645/ns/business-world_business/

- **U.S. N.Y. Stock Exchange** - the American financial market icon, is now 60% owned by the German company Deutsche Borse as of February 2011.
- **Budweiser** - The Great American Lager, majority of its stock to the Belgian-Brazilian brewing company InBev
- **Alka-Seltzer** - Alka-Seltzer was purchased by the German company Bayer AG, now Bayer Schering Pharma AG in 1979.
- **Hellmann's** - In 2000, Best Foods was purchased by Unilever
- **IBM's ThinkPad** Since 2005, the laptop has been manufactured and sold by Lenovo after the company bought IBM's PC division. The ThinkPad brand is still used on Lenovo PCs. Lenovo is the fourth largest personal computer vendor in the world, and the largest in China
- **Ben & Jerry's Ice Cream** - purchased in 2000 by British-Dutch Unilever.
- **7-Eleven** – In 1991 a Japanese company, Ito-Yokado, became the majority shareholder of the once Texas-based franchise.
- **Popsicle brand** - In 1989 it was purchased by Good Humor, another former American company now owned by Unilever.
- **Woman's Day Magazine** - first published in 1931. By 1988, the magazine became the property of Hachette Filipacchi Médias, S.A., which is the largest magazine publisher in the world and is based in France.
- **Purina** - founded in St. Louis, Missouri, in 1894. In 2001 the company became part of Swiss brand giant, Nestle.
- **Gerber** - founded in Fremont, Michigan in 1927. Between 1994 and 1996, several mergers led to eventually becoming part of Swiss pharmaceutical giant, Novartis. The brand sells more than 80% of the American baby food market.
- **Vaseline** - most famous brand of petroleum. In 1987, Vaseline's parent company was purchased by British/Dutch conglomerate Unilever N.V.
- **Lucky Strike Cigarettes** - founded in Richmond, Virgina in 1871, today owned and distributed by British American Tobacco, the world's second largest tobacco company.
- **Firestone Tires** - Firestone Tire and Rubber Company, started in 1900 in Akron, Ohio. In 1988, after a decade of extreme financial hardship, the company sold to the Japanese Bridgestone Corporation.
- **Car and Driver Magazine** - founded in New York City under the title Sports Cars Illustrated in 1955. Today it is owned by the French Hachette Filipacchi Médias

Another interesting list of foreign ownership may be found on the website: www.sourcewatch.org/index.php?title=Foreign_ownership_of_U.S._corporations

The problem is not just a takeover of corporate America; it is a takeover of U.S. real estate market as well:

Remark 5.1: *New York Times Reports August 11*: "Flush with capital from its enormous trade surpluses… Chinese banks have poured more than $1 billion into commercial real estate in New York …diversifying beyond U.S. treasuries..." The article goes on to explain that China is also taking away U.S. construction business…" As well China Construction America … has won contracts including Tappan Zee and Alexander Hamilton Bridges, No. 7 subway lines extension and the $91 million Metro North Railroad station at Yankee Stadium."

In order to understand the magnitude of what we term as a foreign take-over, the following article was published in both Economy in Crisis and TradeReform. It explains the detailed information that will help the reader see these facts regarding foreign ownership of U.S revenue-bearing businesses.

5.2 EXHIBIT C-2: Foreign Ownership of U.S. Companies 51% by 2033 with Skyrocketing U.S. Unemployment Projected[108]

Published March 10, 2010, A. Feinberg

Citizens For Equal Trade (CET)[109] is projecting that Foreign Controlled Domestic Corporations (FCDC) will reach 51% as a percentage of the whole by the year 2033, if current trends continue along with large yearly U.S. trade deficits. We project to the 51% point as it is commonly considered a U.S. business take-over amount. This report is based on projections from a 2005 Grant Thornton Report[110] and other related IRS data receipts projected out from 2007[111,112,113] (see Figures 1, 2 and 3 and Tables 5-2 and 5-3). FCDC ownership was already about 18% in 2007 (see census.gov reference) and is now estimated about 22% through 2010 [see Table 5-3]. We provide two different projections in the appendix, one simply by year (Figure 3), and another projection estimated from the correlation to the U.S. trade deficit data (Figure 2) to foreign ownership. The most reasonable (and conservative)

---

[108] http://www.economyincrisis.org/content/foreign-ownership-us-companies-rising, http://www.tradereform.org/2011/03/foreign-ownership-of-u-s-companies-rising/

[109] www.CitizensForEqualTrade.org

[110] 2005 Grant Thornton Report, http://www.reuters.com/article/2008/08/27/us-companies-ownership-usa-idUSN2744743020080827

[111] 2007 Data Sources, www.census.gov/compendia/statab/2011/tables/11s1291.pdf

[112] 2007 Graphical data: www.bea.gov/newsreleases/international/intinv/2008/pdf/intinv07.pdf

[113] Related IRS data, Foreign-Owned Domestic Corporations with Total Receipts of $500 Million or More, www.irs.gov/taxstats/bustaxstats/article/0,,id=106632,00.html

estimate appears to be related to trade deficit data rather than by year. The trade deficit is a measure of how much more foreigners own of us than we do of them and is now at $8 trillion[114] through 2010 (Table 5-3). The factor of foreign ownership is found to be about 1.8 times the trade deficit amount (Figure 2) and currently helps enable foreign ownership at a rate of about 1.25% per year. Although it is unlikely this factor will keep up, until data show otherwise, it is our best estimate as recent statistics are hard to find.

Furthermore, using a reported 2009 employment rate by FCDC of only 3.5%[115] proportioned to their rather large FCDC estimated ownership in 2009 of about 21% (Table 5-3), the data appears to indicate that U.S. unemployment could skyrocket to over 35% by 2033. A scalable unemployment model for this estimate was used and is provided in Appendix A.4 of this article. The reader is cautioned that since this is a scalable projection, it primarily serves as a crude estimate of the U.S. foreign business employment position over time. Yet, such crude estimates are helpful to alert citizens of this projected plausible crisis.

The likely implications are:

- *51% Foreign control of U.S. business revenue bearing assets in the not too distant future (~25 years)*
- *Transfer of U.S. separation of wealth to foreigners*
- *Major reduction in U.S. consumer spending due to FCDC increases*
- *Excessive unemployment (>35%)*
- *Uncertainty of the business future for Americans*

Spurring this report is the recent unthinkable German acquisition of the U.S. N.Y. Stock exchange[116]. Like China, Germans have large trade surplus U.S. dollars to invest, and they want real tangible U.S. assets with their trade deficit profits.

At what point will America ask the unthinkable question, *"If foreigners could own 51% of all U.S. business by 2033, will this still be a country owned by Americans and governed by them?"*

The trade deficit started in 1971 at about $0.0013 trillion (see our census.gov refer-

---

[114] Trade Deficit data - www.census.gov/foreign-trade/statistics/historical/gands.pdf

[115] A Lifeline Not Made in the U.S.A, M. Maynard, October 17, 2009, www.nytimes.com/2009/10/18/business/18excerpt.html

[116] 8) February 15, 2011, It's official: Germans buy NYSE in $10B deal, www.crainsnewyork.com/article/20110215/FREE/110219927

ence). It accumulated to about $1 trillion just before the start of NAFTA. Since the Free Trade agreements with NAFTA in 1992 and China in 2000, the trade deficit has accumulated to $8 trillion (see our census.gov reference) through 2010 (Table 5-3). During that time, FCDC were 13.9% (see grant Thornton Report Ref.) as a percentage of the whole on U.S. corporations where total assets at foreign owned companies increased to $9.2 trillion in 2005, up from $8.0 trillion in 2004, with $12.01 trillion reported in 2007. This was more than three times the 1996 total of $3 trillion. Foreign-owned assets totaled just $37 billion in 1971 when foreign companies owned 1.3% of all corporate U.S. assets at the start of the trade deficit.

Table 5-2 *Key Findings of Our Projected Report*

Year	Projected Foreign ownership Trillions $	Total Trade Deficit Trillions $	U.S. % Foreign Owned Business	% U.S. Citizens employed by FCDC	% U.S. Citizens Employed by U.S. business Owners	U.S. Unemployment Projection
2033	38.7	21	50.8%	8.6%	53%	36%

The "Trade Deficit Trojan Horse" Effect

We have seen that lack of oversight has cost the U.S. government dearly in the Great Recession on the mortgage crisis. In the case of the trade deficit, the lack of oversight is much worse. Not enough studies like the 2005 Grant Thornton report are available. Certainly, there are no studies that project employment rate due to increasing FCDC assets. This, when combined with U.S. owned assets increasing abroad due to offshoring and other reasons (see Figure 1) could severely challenge U.S. employment. Furthermore, it is well known that foreigners not only cheat in free trade but they also cheat when it comes to reporting their U.S. income taxes[117] which happens to be the main way we have to understand FCDC ownership. Therefore, it is difficult to know what the actual foreign ownership in our country really is. The U.S. will wake up one day in the not too distant future (25 years or less) and find that foreigners have taken control over our industry and our employment. As we may end up defaulting on our foreign-owned government bonds, and are losing control over U.S. corporations to foreigners, it will be clear, we will have lost the war without a bullet being fired. We are becoming defenseless as we fight battles overseas. We coin the term "Trade Deficit Trojan Horse" here due to what is occurring. Readers should understand the connection, and become aware that the trade deficit

---

[117] 9) Tax breaks for multinational corporations, www.ctj.org/hid_ent/part-2/part2-3.htm

also causes national debt (see Chapters 3 and 4). The "twin deficits" (trade deficit and national debt), are highly correlated with the trade deficit found to cause large increases in the large national debt (as described in Chapter 4). It is clear that Congress is distracted and has little understanding of the need for balanced trade. Yet the trade deficit is the biggest threat to our economy, and if left unchanged, it will destroy America's future in less than 25 years.

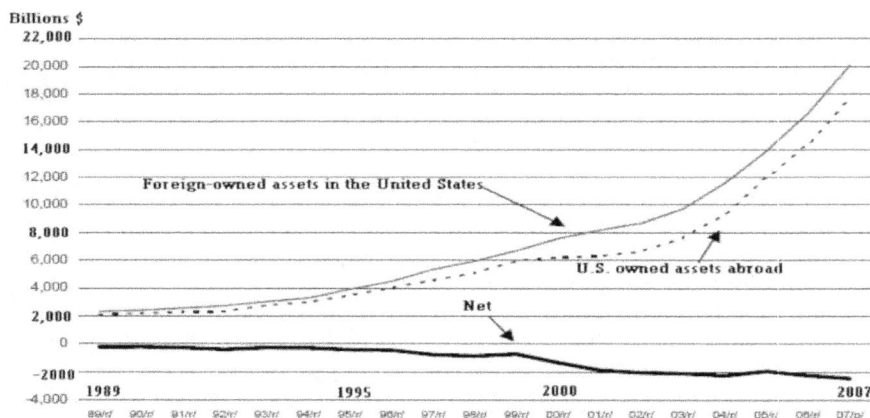

Figure 1 *Foreign-owned assets in the U.S. and U.S. owned assets abroad[118] including securities*

Appendix of Exhibit C-2

Foreign-Controlled Domestic Corporation Asset Projections

A.1 Key Available Data:

The key for information on Foreign-Controlled Domestic Corporations (FCDC) ownership can be found in the Grant Thornton report and other IRS data[119,120,121,122]. Here it is reported that FCDC owned 13.9% of all assets reported from corporation income tax returns of $9.2 trillion in the U.S. in 2005. This is up from $8.0 trillion in 2004. This amount of FCDC ownership is more than three times the 1996 total of $3 trillion. Another report[123] showed FCDC assets at $12.01 trillion in 2007. Foreign-owned assets totaled just $37 billion in 1971 when foreign companies owned 1.3% of

---

[118] 2007 Graphical data: www.bea.gov/newsreleases/international/intinv/2008/pdf/intinv07.pdf

[119] 2005 Grant Thornton Report, www.reuters.com/article/2008/08/27/us-companies-ownership-usa-idUSN2744743020080827

[120] 2007 IRS Data Sources, www.census.gov/compendia/statab/2011/tables/11s1291.pdf

[121] 2007 Graphical data: www.bea.gov/newsreleases/international/intinv/2008/pdf/intinv07.pdf

[122] Related IRS data, Foreign-Owned Domestic Corporations with Total Receipts of $500 Million or More, www.irs.gov/taxstats/bustaxstats/article/0,,id=106632,00.html

[123] www.census.gov/compendia/statab/2011/tables/11s1291.pdf

all corporate U.S. assets at the start of the trade deficit[124]. (Note in 2008 the total U.S. assets were about $188 trillion[125]. Therefore, far less of these U.S. assets are apparently IRS revenue bearing. Below we present two models in A.2 and A.3 of the available data. Both are in reasonable agreement.

A.2 Projection of Foreign Growth in U.S. to 51% Ownership - Model 1 & 2 Foreign Growth

Table 5-3 provides the key estimates. Each column is explained separately below to help the reader.

Table 5-3 Reported (Gray Italic) and Projected Trade Deficit and U.S. Foreign Ownership*

Year	Projected Total Trade Deficit in Trillions $	Foreign ownership $Trillions Model 1	Foreign ownership $Trillions Model 2	U.S Projected Asset Growth Rate at 0.5% per year in Trillions $	Projected % Foreign ownership from Model 1	Projected % U.S. owner- ship from Model 1
1971	0.0013	0.037 (Ref. 2)	0.7			
1996	1.45	3 (Ref. 2)	2.7			
2004	4.26	8 (Ref. 2)	8.3			
2005	4.98	9.2 (Ref. 2)	9.2	66.20	13.9%	86.1%
2006	5.74	10.7	10.1	66.53	16.1%	83.9%
2007	6.44	12.01 (Ref. 3)	11.1	66.86	18.0%	82.0%
2008	7.14	13.3	12.0	67.20	19.7%	80.3%
2009	7.52	14.0	13.1	67.53	20.7%	79.3%
2010	8.02	14.9	14.1	67.87	21.9%	78.1%
2011	8.6	15.9	15.2	68.21	23.3%	76.7%
2012	9.1	16.9	16.4	68.55	24.7%	75.3%
2013	9.7	18.0	17.5	68.89	26.1%	73.9%
2014	10.3	19.0	18.8	69.24	27.5%	72.5%
2015	10.8	20.0	20.0	69.59	28.8%	71.2%
2016	11.4	21.1	21.3	69.93	30.1%	69.9%
2017	12.0	22.1	22.6	70.28	31.5%	68.5%

---

[124] 2005 Grant Thornton Report, www.reuters.com/article/2008/08/27/us-companies-ownership-usa-idUSN2744743020080827
[125] Total Assets of the U.S. Economy $188 Trillion, 13.4xGDP, J. Rutledge, May 24, 2009, http://rutledgecapital.com/2009/05/24/total-assets-of-the-us-economy-188...

2018	12.5	23.2	24.0	70.63	*32.8%*	67.2%
2019	13.1	24.2	25.4	70.99	*34.1%*	65.9%
2020	13.7	25.2	26.8	71.34	*35.4%*	64.6%
2021	14.2	26.3	28.3	71.70	*36.6%*	63.4%
2022	14.8	27.3	29.8	72.06	*37.9%*	62.1%
2023	15.4	28.3	31.4	72.42	*39.1%*	60.9%
2024	15.9	29.4	33.0	72.78	*40.3%*	59.7%
2025	16.5	30.4	34.6	73.14	*41.6%*	58.4%
2026	17.0	31.4	36.3	73.51	*42.8%*	57.2%
2027	17.6	32.5	38.0	73.88	*43.9%*	56.1%
2028	18.2	33.5	39.7	74.25	*45.1%*	54.9%
2029	18.7	34.5	41.5	74.62	*46.3%*	53.7%
2030	19.3	35.6	43.4	74.99	*47.4%*	52.6%
2031	19.9	36.6	45.2	75.37	*48.6%*	51.4%
2032	20.4	37.6	47.1	75.74	*49.7%*	50.3%
2033	21.0	38.7	49.0	76.12	*50.8%*	49.2%

* Highlighted numbers are data points, other numbers are projected.

Column 2 Trade Deficit Projection Method:
The Cumulative trade deficit in Column 2 was estimated based on the average trade deficit over the last 10 years[126]. The average trade deficit was $0.564 Trillion per year. Therefore, 2010 was the last reported trade deficit and $0.564 Trillion has been added yearly to accumulate the trade deficit to a projected $21 trillion by 2033.

Column 3and 4 Foreign Ownership Projection Methods:
Column 3 projections use correlation results with the trade deficit. Column 4 estimates use known data by year plotted and projected using a polynomial method, to provide future estimates. More details are provided below.

Column 3 Foreign Ownership Projection Method:
Foreign ownership in Column 3 for Model 1 was estimated based on the known increase in foreign owner ship in the years 1971, 1996, 2004, 2005 and 2007 reported in the Grant Thornton report[127] and other IRS related data[128] for 2007. These five data points shown in Column 3 rows 1-4 and 6, were then plotted against the cumulative trade deficit values in their respective years and are shown in Figure 2. A

---

[126] Trade Deficit data - www.census.gov/foreign-trade/statistics/historical/gands.pdf

[127] 2005 Grant Thornton Report, www.reuters.com/article/2008/08/27/us-companies-ownership-usa-idUSN2744743020080827

[128] 2007 IRS Data Sources, www.census.gov/compendia/statab/2011/tables/11s1291.pdf

linear relationship is observed with a high correlation. This linear relationship indicates the trade deficit is enabling foreign ownership as anticipated. The linear re-regression Model 2 observed is:

Foreign Ownership in Trillions $ = 1.833 x Trade Deficit + 0.17

The graph and data fit to the points are shown below along with the 95% tight confidence bounds. The five data points are highly correlated with $R^2=0.9985$ yielding a correlation of 99.92%. Data justifies a time lag analysis. However, not enough data was currently available. It seems unlikely that foreign ownership will keep up at this rate. We apologize for not having additional data points after 2007 to improve the trend analysis.

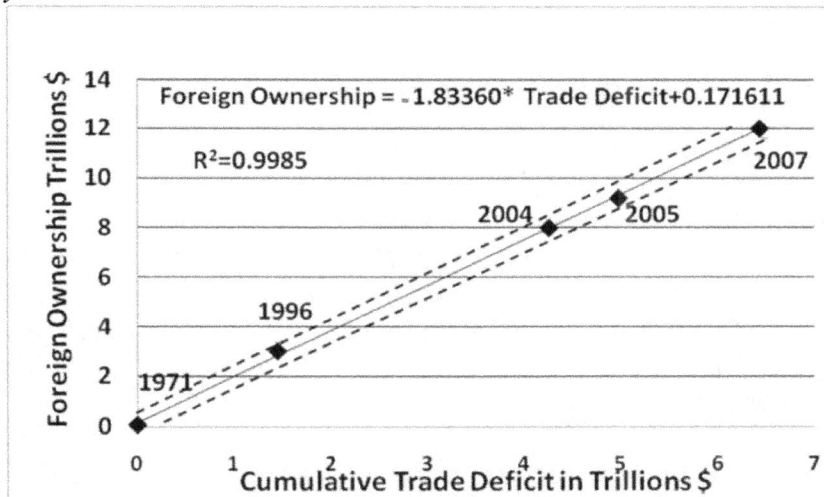

Figure 2 *Linear regressions of FCDC assets vs. cumulative trade deficit data*

A.3 Column 4 Model 2: Foreign Growth – Yearly Model
This is a simple model of just plotting the available foreign ownership asset data by year and fitting it. Model 2 uses the same data available in column3 rows 2-5 and 7, in the years 1971, 1996, 2004, 2005 and 2007 reported in the Grant Thornton report[129] and other IRS related data[130] for 2007. The "Available Data" is then plotted by year in Figure 3. A number of different fits to the data were tried. The exponential function provided a reasonable fit but was overly aggressive in the projection. The polynomial gave the best overall fit although as you can see there are some negative

---

[129] 2005 Grant Thornton Report, www.reuters.com/article/2008/08/27/us-companies-ownership-usa-idUSN2744743020080827
[130] 2007 IRS Data Sources, www.census.gov/compendia/statab/2011/tables/11s1291.pdf

ownership values before 1990. The model is also very sensitive to the coefficient values which require numerous decimal places. The results of the model in terms of projections are shown in Column 4. We see Model 2 is more aggressive than Model 1 but still in the same ballpark. Model 2 shows that in the year 2033 FCDC asset ownership will be around $49 trillion, while Model 2 is about $38.7 trillion. Both are anticipated to be over 51% of all revenue producing assets at that time where U.S. asset revenue bearing ownership reduction is estimated in Column 7.

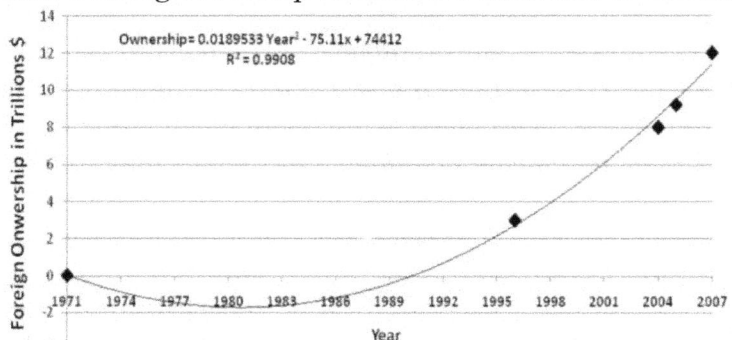

Ownership= 0.0189533 Year² - 75.11x + 74412
$R^2 = 0.9908$

Figure 3 *Polynomial fit to the available data by year*

Column 5: U.S Projected Asset Growth Rate
The first data point in this column $66.2 trillion is estimated from the Grant Thornton report. The report noted that FCDC "foreign-controlled domestic corporations" were 13.9% of all assets reported. This found from U.S. corporation income tax returns of $9.2 trillion in 2005. Therefore, if 13.9% represents $9.2 trillion then we note the whole is $66.2 trillion.

The U.S. asset revenue bearing growth rate is not easy to estimate. We used 0.5% year over year. The rest of the rows in column 5 were then projected based on this growth factor.

Column 6 Percent of U.S. Foreign Assets and Ownership Projection Method:
This column is simply Column 3 divided by Column 5 and taken as a percent.

Column 7 Percent of U.S. Ownership Projection Method:
This is just 100% minus Column 6

A.4 U.S. Unemployment Projection Scalable Model
There is every indication that foreign ownership of U.S. businesses reduces U.S. employment as foreigners run businesses from afar, outsource the U.S. workforce, or merge with their own companies and downsize and bring in their own employees. As well from Figure 1, U.S. businesses are also acquiring more and more assets over-

seas either due to outsourcing or new acquisitions. Offshoring also ships jobs over-seas. This combination of U.S. foreign ownership and U.S. business offshoring is projected to create a tendency for U.S. unemployment to skyrocket. This will also reduce government revenues and likely cause a U.S. crisis.

Scalable Unemployment Model
The New York Times in 2009[131] boasted foreign employment was some 3.5% of the U.S. workforce. What the article failed to mention was that in 2009, foreigners owned approximately 20.7% of all U.S. revenue bearing assets (see Table 5-3). Pro-portionately, this is a terrible U.S. employment rate by FCDC businesses. Here is what this would scale up to by 2033.

2010 Statistics
First we obtain an estimate of the U.S. 2010 business employment rate. About 9.6% is the 2010 unemployment rate, 3.71% foreign employment rate, about 2% Govern-ment employment rate, then U.S. business employment rate is estimated as,

2010 U.S. Business Employment = 100%-9.6%-3.71%-2%=84.7%

(9.6% is 2010 year end unemployment number, 3.71% expected 2010 foreign em-ployment{=3.5x21.9/20.7, see Table 5-3, 2010), 2% government employment rate)

By 2033 foreigners are projected here to own 51%. Scaling the 2009 number up we obtain

FCDC employment percent in 2033= 3.5% x 51% / 20.7% =8.62%
(3.5% is 2009 FCDC employment, 20.7% is the FCDC 2009 ownership number, 51% is their projected ownership in 2033)

U.S. Employment 2033 = 84.69% x 49% / 78.08% = 53.14%
(84.69% is the U.S. 2010 estimated employment number, 78.08% is the estimated U.S. businesses assets in 2010, 49% is the projected U.S. business assets in 2033 since foreigners are projected to own 51% by then.)

If government employment stays the same at 2% then the anticipated unemployment in 2033 would be

---

[131] A Lifeline Not Made in the U.S.A, M. Maynard, October 17, 2009, www.nytimes.com/2009/10/18/business/18excerpt.html

Projected U.S. Unemployment in 2033 = 100-2%-8.62%-53.14%=36.2%

Of course this is a crude scalable model. There are many variables not taken into account such as GDP growth factor, government spending on job creation, and U.S. companies shipping even more jobs overseas, etc. Nevertheless, the actual number is not as important as the fact that unemployment will be scaling upward due to FCDC asset allocation.

5.3 EXHIBIT C-3: Analysis of Internal Revenue Service (IRS) data from Grant Thornton LLP

This information provided is nicely summarized in a Reuter's article.

EXHIBIT B-3 Reuters Aug 2008: Foreign ownership of U.S. companies jumps

"Foreign ownership of U.S. companies more than doubled from 1996 to 2005 measured by revenue and more than tripled as measured by assets, according to an analysis of U.S. tax data released on Wednesday.

The analysis of Internal Revenue Service (IRS) data from Grant Thornton LLP, the U.S. member firm of audit, tax and consulting organization Grant Thornton International Ltd, showed total receipts at "foreign-controlled domestic corporations" rose 13 percent to $3.5 trillion in 2005 from $3.1 trillion in 2004...."

The full article is provided in the following web reference:

www.reuters.com/article/2008/08/27/us-companies-ownership-usa-idUSN2744743020080827.

6

U.S. TRADE DEFICIT POLICY SUPPORTS ORGANIZED CRIMES

If trade were balanced it would severely reduce organized trade deficit crimes. For example, adopting the 2006 Warren Buffett proposal of import certificates[132] would mean that importers would have to purchase the certificate to sell their products in the U.S. This, of course, is only one scenario of possible methods to balance trade. However, under this scenario three things would occur to reduce trade crimes: 1) the importer would need another level of legal paper work to bring in their product, 2) this is an added cost to an illegitimate trade product making it harder to occur, and 3) the serious organized crime of currency manipulation would be stopped dead as well. China's goal in currency manipulation is to create a Chinese trade surplus, which would not be allowed with a balanced trade policy. Japan, too, is guilty of currency manipulation that has severely hurt the U.S. auto industry. These crimes are covered in this chapter.

Simply put, balanced trade is to the trade deficit's organized crimes as the end of prohibition was for the underworld's sales of alcohol.

If you are an American manufacturer interested in working with China, you should heed the warning signs provided in this chapter. The evidence is overwhelming. China has proven itself to be a highly dishonest trading partner. No one really knows if this is an aggressive politically motivated trading policy by Beijing or not. Nevertheless, the U.S. Congress is in fact having quite a difficult time in figuring out what to do about the high trading crimes. We report here that serious measures are in the making. As a potential manufacturer, you may wish to think twice in working with a dishonest trad-

---

[132] http://en.wikipedia.org/wiki/Import_Certificates

ing country.

6.1 Currency Manipulation by China

Currency manipulation is the highest form of organized crime as it is an intentional crime by a foreign government. China's currency manipulation is well recognized by economists and Congress. The best estimates show that the Chinese yuan is undervalued by at least 35% to 40%[133], which makes U.S. goods at least 35% more expensive in China and makes Chinese goods artificially cheap in the United States and around the world. As a result, U.S. imports from China have soared and U.S. exports to China *and the rest of the world* have been suppressed.

There is an effort to pass The Currency Reform for Fair Trade Act of 2011. The Senate passed H.R. 639 currency bill, with a strong bipartisan vote. However, the House is still working to complete the passage.

Currency manipulation literally steals jobs as it robs U.S. GDP growth. We offer the next article as Exhibit D-1, which estimates that 2.1 million jobs were lost due to currency manipulation.

6.1.1 Exhibit D-1: Currency Manipulation Cost 2.1 of 3 Million Lost Trade Deficit Jobs
Posted in Trade Reform and Economy in Crisis, Dr. Alec Feinberg, Citizens For Equal Trade Estimate, June 2011[134, 135]

Exports support jobs in the United States, while imports displace them. The key net effect of the U.S. trade deficit is job losses. Some of the trade deficit is created by currency manipulation and this turns out in our estimate as a major contributor. Citizens for Equal Trade estimates that currency manipulation is responsible for 2.1 million jobs lost or 2/3 of the total job losses related to the trade deficit that now total about 3 million through 2010. We use here a GDP (Gross Domestic Product) job productivity approach to make this estimate.

Jobs Lost Due to the Trade Deficit Estimate
As a verification point, we will first estimate job losses due to the trade deficit using 5 year averages and compare it to an Economic Policy Institute (EPI) estimate through 2010. From Chapter 4, Section 4.3 we noted that the trade deficit jobs lost were

---

[133] http://www.epi.org/page/-/pdf/ib283.pdf
[134] www.economyincrisis.org/content/currency-manipulation-cost-21-3-million-lost-trade-deficit-jobs-0
[135] http://www.tradereform.org/2011/06/currency-manipulation-cost-2-1-of-3-million-lost-trade-deficit-jobs/

$270,000,000,000//$90,000=3 Million jobs lost due to the trade deficit

EPI claimed about 3 million[136] job losses though 2010 (they noted between 2001 and 2008, 2.4 million jobs were lost or displaced, with an average, 345,500 jobs per year, which would yield about 3 million though 2010). This provides a verification point as a good verification check for using this method to roughly estimate the impact of trade deficit job loss.

Jobs Lost Due to Currency Manipulation Estimate
Next let's look at the effect of jobs lost due to currency manipulation.

Fred Bergsten of the Peterson Institute estimates China's currency manipulation costs the United States 1.4 percentage points in GDP annually[137]. The average amount of 1.4% over the last 5 years equates to about $190 billion per year. The job loss estimate is using this method,

$190,000,000,000/$90,000=2.1 million lost jobs due to China's currency manipulation over the years.

From this estimate we see that about 2/3 of the jobs lost in trade deficit activities is due to currency manipulation.

The 2010 unemployment was about 9.6% or about 14.8 million people out of work. This means that unemployment could have been reduced by 2.1 million people down to 12.7 million total unemployed giving an approximate unemployment rate of 8.2%, a reduction of 1.4%. This is quite significant.

Balanced Trade Best Method to Stop Currency Manipulation and Other Issues?
Congress is proposing a Currency Reform for Fair Trade Act of 2011[138]. This should have far reaching capability to control the currency manipulation problems. However, Citizens for Equal Trade believes a better way that would stop not only currency manipulation but all trading violations and save America from the trade deficit train wreck is to balance trade. This also would not violate the WTO

---

[136] www.epi.org/publications/entry/bp260/, Unfair China Trade Costs Local Jobs, Robert E. Scott , March 2010
[137] www.economicpopulist.org/content/chinas-currency-manipulation-makes-amer..., China's Currency Manipulation Makes America See Red, Robert Oak , September 2010
[138] www.americanmanufacturing.org/blog/alliance-american-manufacturing-state..., Alliance for American Manufacturing statement on introduction of new China currency bill, scapozzola, February 2011

agreement and would be the best corrective action. First, it would force improvements in our illogical energy policy. For example, we should be seeking natural gas vehicles initially in the government fleet to start getting us off oil its dependency. Second, the serious organized crime of currency manipulation by China and other countries would be stopped dead. China's goal in currency manipulation is to create a Chinese trade surplus. This causes a good portion of the U.S. goods trade deficit (about $190 billion - see last section), which would not be allowed with a balanced U.S. trade policy. As well, U. S. corporations consistently lose billions of dollars in intellectual property and unfair trade every year due to patent, copyright, trademark piracy infringements, product counterfeiting, product subsidies, hidden foreign trade barriers, violations in foreign anti-dumping agreements, currency manipulation, and so forth. For example, one estimate is that 7% of all global trade is related to counterfeit goods[139]. All this would go away in a balanced-seeking trade requirement. Not to mention a key problem that most people do not understand. That is the trade deficit cause a good portion of the U.S. national debt[140,141].

6.2 Intellectual Property Losses

U. S. corporations consistently lose billions of dollars in intellectual property loses. A CNBC Special was aired in July 2010 that cited 7% of all global trade is related to counterfeit goods.

Remark 6.1: *"There's an undeclared war being waged in the United States at our ports, on our borders and even in cyberspace. From shoes and watches to prescription drugs and military equipment the business of counterfeit goods is booming, robbing U.S. businesses, costing Americans jobs and bankrolling terrorism... Among the most lethal counterfeits are medicines. Imposter products including cough syrup and baby formula have killed thousands worldwide...and the death toll continues to rise. And, with patients using the Internet to find deals on pharmaceuticals the risk is even higher. In fact, according to the World Health Organization, more than half of all drugs purchased from unregistered online pharmacies are counterfeit."[142]*

6.2.1 Exhibit D-2: Counterfeit Goods – The Largest Underground Industry in the World

---

[139] www.cnbc.com/id/38131788/CNBC_S_CRIME_INC_COUNTERFEIT_GOODS_WILL_PREMIER

[140] Islam, M., and Rahimian, E. (2005). "An Empirical Analysis of the Relationship Between the Budget Deficit and the Trade Deficit", Journal of Academy of Business and Economics, 5-2, 1542

[141] http://citizensforequaltrade.org/US%20Trade%20Def%20Causes%20National%20..., U.S. Trade Deficit Creates Budget Deficit –NAFTA and China Causality Study, , A. Feinberg April 2011

[142] www.cnbc.com/id/38021306/CNBC_PRESENTS_CRIME_INC_COUNTERFEIT_GOODS

The following summary was provided by CNBC on their July 2010 show[143].

Fake handbags, watches, shoes and perfumes... the business of Counterfeit Goods is the largest underground industry in the world. Hundreds of billions of dollars are generated while sapping the economy, putting lives in jeopardy, and funding organized crime in the process.

CNBC's "Crime Inc.: Counterfeit Goods," takes viewers on a rare look inside a global crime spree, where the goods are produced and confiscated in a world of high-risk and high-reward.

<u>At around 7% of all global trade, Counterfeit Goods are a big business with low overhead.</u>

Table 6-1 CNBC Top 10 Reported Counterfeited Categories

Category	Value - Source: U.S Customs & Boarder Protection	Example
Toys/Electronic Games	2009 Domestic Seizure Value: $5.50 million Percent of Total Seizures: 2%	Genuine and counterfeit Barbie dolls
Jewelry	2009 Domestic Seizure Value: $10.50 million Percent of Total Seizures: 4%	Counterfeit Dior jewelry
Pharmaceuticals	2009 Domestic Seizure Value: $11.06 million Percent of Total Seizures: 4%	Viagra
Media	2009 Domestic Seizure Value: $11.09 million Percent of Total Seizures: 4%	Pop and rap music CDs
Computers/Hardware	2009 Domestic Seizure Value: $12.54 million Percent of Total Seizures: 5%	Fake iPhones and other hardware displayed.
Watches/Parts	2009 Domestic Seizure Value: $15.53 million Percent of Total Seizures: 6%	Omega watches
Apparel	2009 Domestic Seizure Value: $21.46 million Percent of Total Seizures: 8%	Genuine and counterfeit Adidas and Lacoste shirts.
Handbags/Wallets/ Backpacks	2009 Domestic Seizure Value: $21.50 million Percent of Total Seizures: 8%	Genuine and counterfeit Dior bags.
Consumer Electronics	2009 Domestic Seizure Value: $31.77 million Percent of Total Seizures: 12%	Sony, Nakiva radios
Footwear	2009 Domestic Seizure Value: $ 99.78 million Percent of Total Seizures: 38%	Dior Shoes .

The above table provides an overview of the counterfeited items that CNBC posted on their website in the form of a slide show related to their report.[144]

---

[143] http://www.cnbc.com/id/37824347/

6.2.2 Exhibit D-3: Patent, Copyright and Trademark Piracy, Testimony of Former Senator Gorton – China largest offender

The following was a May 2011 Testimony of former U.S. Senator Slade Gorton before The U.S. China Economic and Security Review Commission hearing on China's intellectual property rights and indigenous innovation policy

"U. S. corporations consistently lose billions of dollars in intellectual property every year due to patent, copyright and trademark piracy and infringement, together with the impacts of Chinese indigenous innovation policies. All in all, not surprisingly, China is the greatest offender.

How to measure these losses presents huge challenges, but let's start with a study by the International Data Corporation. It estimates China's software piracy rate in 2009 to have been 79%, with a value of about $7.6 billion. Another study found direct losses to copyright industries in 2005 to have been on the order of $58 billion in lost output and accompanying lost jobs, earnings and tax revenues. A reasonable assumption might be that China accounts for about 25% of this number, or $14 billion.

We can, of course, take for granted that these losses have been matters of great concern to several American administrations and, therefore, the subject of constant negotiations, the only common feature of which is a lack of success.

And it is, of course, the resulting frustration, coupled with the huge imbalance in our bilateral trade with China that has spawned retaliatory schemes like Senator Schumer's proposal to sanction China's artificial valuation of its currency.

But while I believe that the senator's ideas stem from an appropriate concern over those trade imbalances and unfairness, I do not feel that his approach is likely to succeed.

We should recognize that the control of a nation's own currency to the maximum extent possible is in its clear vital sovereign national interest. One need only reflect on the reaction here in the United States to any Chinese attempt to order us to raise interest rates so as to strengthen the dollar to understand and even to sympathize with China's view on the same subject.

---

[144] http://www.cnbc.com/id/37824359

At the same time, however, the protection of our national intellectual property is clearly a vital national sovereign interest of the United States. We have the sovereign right to adjust our trade policies so as to protect that interest. Unfair trade policies should be met by trade sanctions.

Thus, our protection of that intellectual property having been so ineffectual, I submit to you once again an idea first brought to your attention several months ago by my friend, Leo Hindery.

The United States should impose on all imports from China a goods tariff designed to produce each year 150% of the losses of US intellectual property in the previous year. The GAO (Government Accountability Office) should determine that number, and the policy should continue for as long as that piracy exceeds an appropriate share of US exports to China, say 10%. The policy should be universal, that is to say it should apply equally to all other trading partners the piracy in which exceeds a certain level. The president should be given some, but very little, authority to waive the policy, in whole or in part, upon a determination that it is in our clear national interest to do so.

The goal, of course, is not to produce revenue for the federal treasury, but to reduce intellectual property piracy, and any degree of presidential discretion should be directed at rewarding success in that endeavor.

It will be objected that this policy violates a number of our international trade agreements, as it does, thus allowing retaliatory trade sanctions against US exports to China, though it should be pointed out that Chinese piracy is so extensive as to constitute such violations as well.

True as that right of retaliation is, and perhaps effective in the case of any trading partner with whom we have a trade surplus, it is clear that a China with a $273 billion surplus (2010) with the United States can only lose, and lose big, by any set of tit for tat retaliatory trade sanctions with the United States.

This general proposal does not, of course, answer all relevant questions. Do we treat patent, copyright and trademark piracy and violations in the same fashion? And what about government indigenous innovation policies? To what extent do they differ from trade secret sharing in the normal course of corporate negotiations? And how do we fairly and accurately determine the losses resulting from IP (Intellectual Property) piracy?

Each of these questions is food for examination by this Commission, but the time for decisive action has already passed and we should not wait on the results of future fruitless negotiations.

Stealing of intellectual property is also done on the internet. The following story came out on November 3, 2011 regarding China and Russia Interne Spying.

Remark 6.2: *"Washington - American intelligence agencies, in an unusually blunt public criticism of China and Russia, reported to Congress on Nov. 3, 2011 that those two foreign governments (China and Russia) steal valuable American technology over the Internet as a matter of national policy..."*[145]

6.3 Non-Tariff Trade Barriers by U.S. Trading Partners – China, Japan and Others.

In this section we provide evidence of non-tariff trade barriers that have severely hurt the U.S. businesses including Detroit's auto industry crippling U.S. job creation in Detroit and other industries. We provide evidence of VAT taxes by China which are manipulated and provide an unfair advantage of the U.S. corporate tax system. Perhaps the biggest crime is that most of these crimes would all be stopped with a U.S. balanced trade policy.

6.3.1 Exhibit D-4: Japan's Currency Manipulation helps Topple U.S. Auto Industry and Detroit Jobs

"In 2004, Japan exported to the United States over 1.7 million passenger vehicles and a substantial amount of auto parts worth a total of $46 billion. During the same time, Japan imported just 15,000 passenger vehicles and auto parts from the United States worth a total of $1.8 billion. The market share of Japanese nameplate brands reached over 30% of the total U.S. light vehicle market in 2004—including nearly 40% of passenger cars. In contrast, sales of U.S. nameplates in Japan reached only 2% of the total market....In 2005 automotive imports worth $239 billion of cars, trucks and auto parts, and only exported $98 billion." [146]

"In 2008 the U.S. had a $55.8 billion trade deficit in auto and auto parts with Japan that represented about 8% of our total trade deficit. U.S. exports of autos and auto parts to Japan were almost 27% lower in 2008 than in 2000..."[147]

---

[145] www.nytimes.com/2011/11/04/world/us-report-accuses-china-and-russia-of-internet-spying.html
[146] http://waysandmeans.house.gov/hearings.asp?formmode=printfriendly&id=3798
[147] www.autotradecouncil.org/Upload/W+M%20letter.pdf

Many have suggested that General Motors and Chrysler's failure was a matter of quality, cost, and poor business management. These are certainly some of the issues. Nevertheless, similar to China, there have been accusations of currency manipulation by Japan that have potentially hurt Detroit auto sales. A weaker yen in competitive years (2000–2005) was described as a key issue in a 2005 in a statement by M. Mohatarem, a chief economist for GM to the House, Ways, and Means Committee in 2005.

Evidence D-4: September 2005—"Japan's weak yen policy has given its exporters a huge subsidy and competitive advantage in the U.S. market, causing significant harm to U.S. manufacturers. One clear sign that a country is manipulating its currency is a substantial increase in its foreign currency reserves, which occurs as it buys and holds dollars. Japan has seen a massive increase in its foreign currency reserves since 2001, growing from $344.8 billion in July 2000 to $840 billion in July 2005… Japan's artificially weak currency provides a significant per-vehicle cost advantage that amounts to an outright annual subsidy of between $3,000 for small car to $12,000 for a luxury sedan or SUV for every vehicle exported to the United States. Cars produced here by Japanese companies also benefit heavily from this subsidy because of their high use of imported parts and components."[148]

There is little doubt in Detroit's mind that free trade has been a nightmare. Chrysler's bankruptcy and GM's turmoil is a painful occurrence that many believe is due in part to an imperfect free trade situation and a clear failure to implement reliability economics. It is another lack of oversight by the U.S. government to ignore the warning signs.

"From 2000–2005, subsidized by an artificially weak yen funded by $420 billion in Japanese government currency interventions, Japan's automakers have exported an annual average of 1.8 million cars and trucks into the United States, 13% higher than the average from 1996–2000." [149]

The automakers have had some success with Congress to make changes.

March 28, 2007—"Automakers Endorse Japan Currency Manipulation Act; Applaud Stabenow... "[150]

However, the yen was back down in May of 2009 to its lowest level in at least nine years. The automakers still struggle for fair trade. In a letter to President Obama, written by many representatives dated March 2009, strong problems persist:

---

[148] waysandmeans.house.gov/hearings.asp?formmode=printfriendly&id=3798
[149] waysandmeans.house.gov/hearings.asp?formmode=printfriendly&id=3798
[150] www.motortrend.com/features/newswire/27417/index.html

"Japan also continues to block imports of U.S. auto parts using a combination of non-tariff barriers. For example, Japan levies an annual automobile tax that increases by engine size, discriminating against many U.S. vehicles. Japan also continues to restrict severely the number of garages that can perform service repairs through its "certified garage" and "designate garage" system. The vast majority (80%) of aftermarket parts and service sales is controlled by dealerships affiliated with Japanese OEMs which are inclined to buy and sell auto parts from closely related Japanese auto companies."[151]

Unfortunately, now much of the damage is done. The U.S. auto industry is in harsh turmoil and hundreds of thousands of jobs have been lost. Part of the problem is the difficulty the automakers have had working with a Congress that is slow to respond over the years to the warning signs. Yet in a time of crisis, in less than six months, Congress has responded with billions in taxpayer bailout money.

"Adding the $25 billion loan program (for Car R&D) to the $85 billion in TARP funds that have already been earmarked for the auto industry brings the total in taxpayer aid going to auto companies to $110 billion."[152]

It is clear that this is a case of putting out fires with tax payer's bailout funds rather than having been proactive in fighting for balanced trade policies back in 2005. All this could have been prevented with a balanced trade policy. As we have stated, currency manipulation would not occur with a balance trade policy. Auto bailouts might not have occurred if a reliability economics team existed, as they might have stopped the problems early and acting in a proactive manner.

6.3.2 Exhibit D-5: Foreign VAT Tax versus the U.S. Corporate tax - A U.S. competitive disadvantage

Virtually all other countries have a consumption tax, like a Value Added Tax (VAT) except for the U.S. The average VAT tax level is 17%. The tax is border adjustable because foreigners manipulate it and charge incoming goods with the tax, and pay their exporting companies a 17% tax rebate when exporting goods. It can be like a tariff if not equally charged to importers and exporters and then acts like a "border adjustable" tax (see Exhibit below). In general, the VAT tax is WTO legal. However, the U.S. corporate tax has no similar adjustments. The following article excerpt was published in Barrons and re-published in tradereform.org in 2008[153]

---

[151] www.autotradecouncil.org/Upload/W+M%20letter.pdf

[152] www.propublica.org/ion/bailout/item/govt-begins-doling-out-25-billion-in-green-car-loans

[153] http://www.tradereform.org/tag/barrons/

"Taxes on world trade are levied according to a set of rules that penalize the United States for its reliance on corporate income taxes. Under the rules of the World Trade Organization, value-added taxes need not be levied if the taxed goods or services are exported. No such export rebate is allowed for corporate income taxes. If a German car might be liable for $5,000 of value-added tax, its manufacturer would receive the $5,000 back from the tax authorities after driving the car onto a ship bound for the United States. A Honda exported from these shores (U.S.) would carry its share of the manufacturer's corporate income tax across the ocean, with no rebate allowed…"

"The U.S. Congress goes on year after year holding hearings about this inequity, and the U.S. goes on and on running up trade deficits, but nothing is ever done to secure better tax treatment for our exports by substituting a value-added tax for the corporate income tax, or by negotiating equal treatment for both kinds of taxation…"

Another reason that the VAT tax is sanctioned by the WTO is that economists believe it balances out in the value of the currency, so if one country charges it and another does not then it will not cause a competitive advantage. The problem is that in a world of China's currency manipulation, greed, and VAT tax rebates[154], free trade becomes unbalanced and does in fact hurt the U.S. For example, if China charges a VAT tax to U.S. importers and not to their own manufacturers in certain areas like agriculture, it is then a tariff and creates an unfair competitive advantage (see Exhibit D-2-2 below).

We are not in favor of a U.S. VAT tax as it can hurt consumers. Alternately, we would rather see balanced trade required; countries like China could no longer seek to unbalance trade through VAT tax manipulation.

In Exhibit D-5-1, we provide evidence that China gets more than 20% of its government revenue from taxes on imports while the U.S. gets 1.38%. This added to their currency manipulation, their selective VAT taxing and the U.S. corporate tax rate quickly unbalances trade, costs U.S. jobs, creates lost tax revenue, and increases the national debt.

Exhibit D-5-1: How we pay Chinese taxes - 20% of their government revenue from import taxes by Edwin Way in July 2011[155].
"Beijing relies heavily on import taxes. More than 20% of Chinese central government revenue in 2009 was generated from import taxes, while the comparable figure for the U.S. was just 1.4%."

---

[154] www.tradereform.org/2011/07/cpa-white-paper-how-chinas-vat-massively-subsidizes-exports/
[155] www.tradereform.org/2011/07/how-we-pay-chinese-taxes-20-of-their-government-revenue/

"The Chinese impose three major taxes on most imported products: a value-added tax of 17% on imported goods destined for domestic consumption, a variety of consumption taxes and also tariffs which vary by import category and are generally higher on manufactured goods. For example, there is a 45% tariff on motorcycle imports, which is particularly damaging for the US given that the US consistently enjoys a large trade surplus in motorcycles. Chinese value added tax and consumption taxes are typically waived for imported raw materials and imports destined for goods to be exported."

Exhibit D-2-2 – Selective VAT tax tariff example
In a report in March 2011 by the <u>U.S. International Trade Commission</u> entitled, <u>China's Agricultural Trade: Competitive Conditions and Effects on US. Exports</u>[156], their findings showed China's domestic producers were exempt from the VAT while importers were subject to large VAT taxes. The findings were nicely summarized by an article CPA TradeReform:

China uses value added tax to keep out agricultural trade
By Michael Stumo, March 2011.

In the agricultural trade sector, farmers and ranchers are told of the riches they will achieve selling to China. The U.S. International Trade Commission explored the issue and found that the riches will not be soon coming. The article continues and quotes the U.S. International Study -

*...Exemptions to the VAT for China's agricultural sector fall into four categories. Based on the order they fall in the production chain, they are farm inputs, farm sales, processor-imputed VAT, and processor-exempted products. The farm inputs exempt from the VAT include seeds, pesticides, herbicides, agricultural machinery, and some fertilizers. These inputs may add up to as much as one-third of the cost of the crop to the farmer. Because all products from agricultural producers are sold without paying the VAT, buyers (e.g., food processors) of goods from these producers are able to deduct **13 percent** of these inputs' value when calculating the VAT they charge at the next point of sale (processor-imputed VAT). This exemption protects processors, when they source domestically produced food inputs, from paying the VAT that farmers are exempted from paying and also from double payment of the VAT for certain farm inputs that were not VAT-free. The practical effect of this policy, which allows buyers to deduct the VAT that they did not originally pay, is that domestically produced agricultural products gain a cost advantage over competing imported products....*

---

[156] http://www.usitc.gov/publications/332/pub4219.pdf

6.3.3 Exhibit D-6: General WTO Violations

Evidence D-6 provides some general examples of WTO violations by our trading partners on subsidies and trade barriers:

> **Evidence D-6 (continued)**: April 2004—"House Democrats sent a letter to the President after the release of the *National Trade Estimates* report urging President Bush to take immediate action to address the unfair trade barriers standing in the way of U.S. exports.... 'After the loss of almost three million manufacturing jobs since January 2001, and the growing problem of outsourcing in the services sector...The cases include ones involving European subsidies to Airbus, various Japanese and Korean barriers to U.S. exports of autos and auto parts, India's non-tariff barriers on textiles, lack of intellectual property protection by India, and a growing number of areas in which China is not living up to its WTO commitments, such as denial of trading rights and distribution barriers.'"[157]

The below evidence shows how the U.S. is another indication on how the U.S. is unable to maintain fair trade practices or impose penalties, only tally violations.

> **Evidence D-6 (continued)**: April 2007—"Inadequate IPR (Intellectual Property Rights) protections reduce U.S. access to China's market and other countries' markets for such products as films, music, published materials, software, pharmaceuticals, chemicals, information technology, consumer goods, industrial goods, food products, medical devices, electrical equipment, automotive parts, clothing, and footwear, according to the release."[158]

6.4 Exhibit D-7: China Owes the U.S. Trillions of Dollars in Trade Violations

China has driven many U.S. industries to bankruptcy, some of these simply due to competitive wage issues; that is, China is a much lower wage earning country than the U.S. Yet other failures of U.S. industries are questionable. In Chapter 1, Remarks 1.6 and 1.7 are two good examples of the solar industry's failure and the U.S. steel industry being crippled by a rich Chinese government providing subsidies in violation of the WTO agreements. China clearly targeted these U.S. manufacturers to gain dominance in these industries. U.S. industries are supposed to be competing against other global companies, not China's wealthy government. In the solar area it was an apparent trade war with government subsidies. For any chess move that the U.S makes, such as in the solar industry, where Obama tried to subsidize solar companies (see Remark 1.6), China seems to have had an answer with higher subsidies that have driven U.S. solar companies to failure costing thousands of U.S. jobs. Yet the U.S. government is una-

---

[157] www.house.gov/apps/list/press/wm31_democrats/040401bush_admin_remove_unfair_trade.html
[158] http://useu.usmission.gov/Article.asp?ID=08A0ACC7-5916-49E2-B865-0F853252FF0E

ware of these China chess moves until it is too late.

> **Remark 6.3** "*…China's national government policies allow their manufacturers to use trade cheats. For example, there are unbalanced tariffs, such as the 2.5 percent for a car entering America vs. 25 percent for a car coming into China. In addition, the Chinese government requires foreign firms to have a Chinese "partner" company, who maintains the majority interest, takes most of the profits, and has the real control of the company. More seriously, China now requires U. S. companies to share their technology and relocate their R&D centers to China if they want to have access to Chinese markets.*"[159]

America cannot compete and there is not even fair trade with China never mind free trade. However, America holds one true advantage right now. We are the world's biggest customer. It is logical to balance trade, fining countries like China that regularly violate WTO policy, refuse to trade fairly, and cripple U.S. industries.

Many in Congress would be afraid of retaliatory tactics like tariffs or fines. Some inappropriately point to the Smoot-Hawley Tariff Act of 1930 that ended up increasing unemployment due to retaliation by U.S. trading partners. However, this occurred when the U.S. had a trade surplus. With today's trade deficit, the U.S. can win most tariff or fine wars.

China is a terrible trading partner in all areas. Recently (September 5, 2011), China sought to sell arms to Gaddafi according to the CNBC and the NY times.

> **Remark 6.4**: "*In the final weeks of Col. Gaddafi's battle with Libyan rebels, Chinese state companies offered to sell his government large stockpiles of weapons and ammunition in apparent violation of United Nations sanctions…*"[160]

China, our largest trading partner, has proven itself to be highly dishonest. We also refer the reader to the book, *Death by China*[161]. We truly believe that China owes the U.S. trillions of dollars in trade violations. They are also responsible for the illegal trade conducted by their citizens and their organized crimes against U.S. manufacturers. It is unbelievable that Congress does nothing about this and refuses to seek retribution. We should file huge claims against China through the WTO and seek to balance trade and end their trade war-like activity on the U.S. Its actions indicate they more wish to conquer the U.S. than trade with America. Congress seems to have no idea the seriousness of this apparent aggression on the U.S by China.

---

[159] http://www.huffingtonpost.com/michele-nashhoff/what-is-the-secret-behind_1_b_930018.html
[160] www.cnbc.com/id/44395867?par=RSS
[161] See recommended trade reform books – back of this book

7

TRADE DEFICIT COUNTRIES HAVE HIGHER UNEMPLOYMENT

G lobally, free trade produces countries with trade deficits and trade surpluses. Exports support jobs in the United States, while imports displace them. The key net effect of the U.S. trade deficit is job losses. In the past, Free Trade theorists such as Adam Smith and Milton Friedman have asserted that unemployment[162] should be relatively insensitive to the effects of the balance of trade and even that trade deficits can be good for an economy (as discussed in Wikipedia ref.). Here we study the Reliability Economics[163] of the balance of trade data on unemployment. Most of the information comes from an article published in *Economy in Crisis* by the author[164].

7.1 Exhibit E – Trade Deficit Countries Have Higher Unemployment - Study[165]

We present recent data (mostly 2009 and 2010) on the top 25 countries each with a trade deficit or a trade surplus and look to see if and how this influences their unemployment rates. We find a 60 to 72% correlation between the balance of a country's trade and its overall unemployment rate. That is, countries with trade surplus have

---

[162] See Adam Smith and Milton Friedman remarks on the Trade Deficit ideology, http://en.wikipedia.org/wiki/Balance_of_trade

[163] A. Feinberg, The Truth of the Modern Recession, Root Causes and Reliable Solutions, An Introduction to Reliability Economics, WE-Economy Press. www.amazon.com/Truth-Modern-Recession-Reliable Solutions/dp/0615315291

[164] A.Feinberg, Trade Deficit Countries Have Higher Unemployment Rates, Sept 2010. http://economyincrisis.org/content/trade-deficit-countries-have-higher-unemployment-rates–balanced-trade-needed

[165] Original study published at http://economyincrisis.org/content/trade-deficit-countries-have-higher-unemployment-rates–balanced-trade-needed

lower unemployment rates while countries with trade deficits tend to have higher unemployment. Of course, there are many factors that affect unemployment rate besides the balance of trade. For example, unemployment rates are influenced by a country's governmental employment program and their political situation. Thus, here we look at the raw data for this trend. The results indicate that there is an overall pervasive trend in recent trade balance data to the unemployment rate. We use compiled recent data as it is the best leading future indicator compared to prior years. This is a key issue; while obvious to citizens around the world who have lost their jobs to globalization, economists, political leaders, and experts[166] fail to face up to the data that shows trade deficits are harmful to a country's unemployment rate and the overall economy[167]. They perhaps trust economists who are swayed by free trade ideology. In a time of economic global uncertainty, such data should not be ignored by Congress and economists.

Evaluation

Figure 7-1 (from Table 7-1) provides the countries reviewed (top 13 trade surplus and top 12 trade deficit countries). The unemployment rate per country is shown in Figure 7-1[168]. The height of the bar graph provides each country's unemployment rate. At the top of each bar are two printed values indicating the country's trade deficit or surplus. The first number is the trade deficit in billions of U.S. dollars[169] while the second number is the trade deficit as a percent of the country's GDP[170]. The figure is divided with the left side showing countries with trade deficits, while the right side, countries with trade surpluses. Each side is sorted from highest employment rate to lowest. The statistical analysis is shown in Figures 7-2 and 7-3 and discussed in the appendix. In Figures 7-2 and 7-3, recent unemployment rates versus the trade balance (as a percent of GDP) are plotted. It shows a 60% to 72% correlation between the unemployment rate and balance of trade as a percentage of GDP (see Appendix for details). The mathematical relationship found indicates about 20 to 28% of the trade balance (% of GDP) affects the unemployment rate. The statistical chance that this result is in error is very small (lower than 1 in 1000). Thus there can be little debate when looking at this data. In this case with the data presented and the countries selected, the trend is clear,

---

[166] Bloomberg Experts on Fix the Economy (fail to consider the trade deficit in their analysis). www.businessweek.com/magazine/content/10_39/b4196054741296.htm
[167] A. Feinberg, Biggest Threat to America's Future --The U.S. Trade Deficit.
[168] List of Countries by unemployment, http://en.wikipedia.org/wiki/List_of_countries_by_unemployment_rate
[169] Balance of Trade by country, http://en.wikipedia.org/wiki/List_of_sovereign_states_by_current_account_balance
[170]http://en.wikipedia.org/wiki/List_of_sovereign_states_by_current_account_balance

there is a tendency for countries with trade surpluses to have a better employment rate while countries with higher trade deficits tend to suffer greater unemployment.

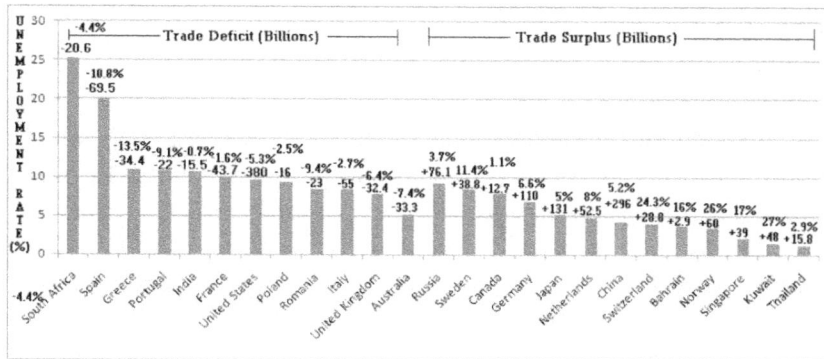

Figure 7-1 Unemployment Rate Versus Top 25 Balance of Trade Countries (recent data[171,172]). Number on top of bar is the trade deficit in billions the second number is the trade deficit as a % of the country's GDP.*Note: Iraq and Saudi Arabia data points removed due to political influences and energy issues to reduce skewing of the data.

Another interesting fact is to look at some of the counties with serious issues such as Greece and the U.S. Greece has the highest trade deficit of -13.5% as a percent of its GDP. The U.S. is in the upper mid area in terms of trade deficit at -5.3% as percent of its GDP. Both countries have serious national debt problems. National debt has been shown to also be highly correlated to the U.S. trade deficit (see Chapter 4, Exhibits B-1, B-2, B-3). It would come as no surprise if this were not part of Greece's national debt problem as well (also see Chapter 1 on the Euro causing trade deficit problems).

Also of interest is that the top non-U.S. trade deficit countries averaged about -$33 billion in trade deficit compared to the U.S. trade deficit of -$380 billion. In other words, the U.S. trade deficit is over 10 times higher than average. China, now the largest U.S. importer "partner," on the other end, has the benefiting surplus of $296 billion in 2009, roughly a factor of about 6 times higher in trade surplus compared to recent averages. Meanwhile China's unemployment rate is 4.3% compared to the U.S. with a 9.6%.

---

[171] List of Countries by unemployment,
http://en.wikipedia.org/wiki/List_of_countries_by_unemployment_rate
[172] Balance of Trade by country,
http://en.wikipedia.org/wiki/List_of_sovereign_states_by_current_account_balance

Conclusion
Here we statistically presented data showing that a root cause of high unemployment is a country's trade deficit. The statistical correlation between a county's unemployment rate and balance of trade ranges between 60 to 72% depending on how the data is looked at (see Chapter Appendix for details). Since the root cause of a trade deficit is a country's global free trade policy, it is clear that a good equal trade policy is essential for balanced global employment. A poor balance of trade will cause suffering for millions of people who seek employment in trade deficit countries all over the globe. On top of the list is the U.S. with the world's largest trade deficit by over a factor of 10 on average compared to the top current trade deficit countries. The U.S. is clearly on a destructive path with this kind of trade deficit behavior. If Congress wishes to seriously address the U.S. unemployment rate, experts and Congress should stop treating the trade deficit like a fact of life and react to the needs of its people. It is clear that the top economies around the world have found their economic solution: keep a high trade surplus to the U.S. Our opinion is that free trade should be replaced globally with a balance of trade policy[173] in order for all economies to properly benefit. Trade deficit countries risk not only high unemployment rates but also large national debts and do put their economies at great risk. In actuality, trade deficit countries that fail, such as Greece, will also eventually cause problems with the global economy.

7.2 Chapter Appendix – Data Analysis
Recent unemployment rates and balance of trade by country are provided in Table 7-1. Here we show the correlation between countries' trade balances (as a percent of GDP) and their unemployment rates.

A basic regression analysis was looked at between Column 2, the Unemployment Rate and Column 4, the Trade Balance (%GDP). The regression graph is shown in Figure 7-2. A 60% correlation was first noted. The relationship found in the regression indicates that the trade balance x 0.28 affects the unemployment rate. The P-value in a Pearson correlation value of 0.001 obtained in the data fit, indicating little chance this data is in error (i.e., 1 chance in a 1000 this result is in error). We note the dotted lines 90% confidence bounds. One more analysis was then performed.

---

[173] www.CitizensForEqualTrade.org

Table 7-1: 2009 Unemployment Rate and Balance of Trade by Country[174,175]

Country	Unemployment Rate	Trade Balance	Trade Deficit (%GDP)
South Africa	25.3	−20.6	-4.4
Spain	20.05	−69.46	-10.8
Greece	11	−34.43	-13.46
Portugal	10.8	−21.987	-9.1
India	10.7	−15.494	-0.65
France	10	−43.67	-1.63
United States	9.6	−380.1	-5.33
Poland	9.4	−15.905	-2.5
Romania	8.4	−23.234	-9.4
Italy	8.4	−55.44	-2.7
United Kingdom	7.8	−32.37	-6.4
Australia	5.1	−33.31	-7.4
Russia	9.2	76.163	3.7
Sweden	8.5	38.797	11.4
Canada	7.9	12.726	1.05
Germany	6.9	109.7	6.6
Japan	5.2	131.2	5
Netherlands	4.8	52.522	8
China	4.3	296.2	5.2
Switzerland	4	28.776	24.3
Bahrain	3.7	2.906	16
Norway	3.5	59.983	25.7
Singapore	2.2	39.157	17.2
Kuwait	1.5	48.039	28.6
Thailand	1.2	15.765	2.9

We see in Figure 7-2, two high outliers with excessive unemployment rates. These were identified as South Africa and Spain (see Table 7-1). These outliers, far from the

---

[174] List of Countries by unemployment,
http://en.wikipedia.org/wiki/List_of_countries_by_unemployment_rate
[175] Balance of Trade by country,
http://en.wikipedia.org/wiki/List_of_sovereign_states_by_current_account_balance

90% confidence lines, were removed. Figure 7-3 regression analysis then resulted. Here we find a 72% correlation between Column 2, the unemployment rate and Column 4 the Trade balance (%GDP). The relationship found in this regression indicates that the Trade Balance x 0.193 affects the Unemployment Rate. Other analyses are possible. However, this provides a good indication of the trend.

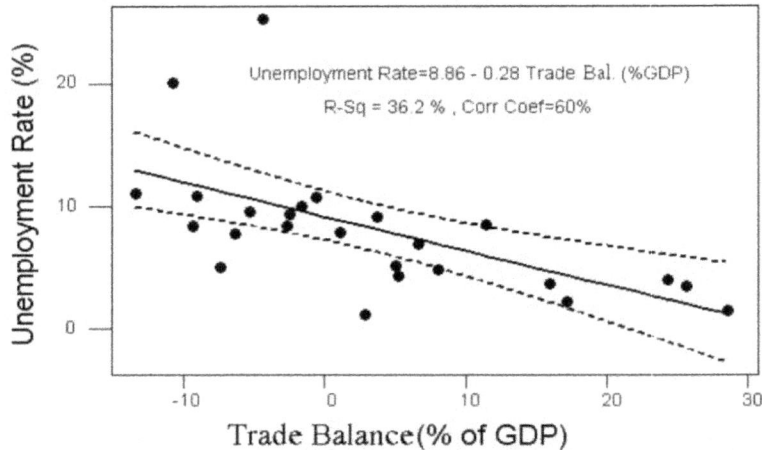

Figure 7-2 Regression analysis of Table 7-1 between Column 2, the Unemployment Rate and Column 4, the Trade Deficit (%GDP). Dotted lines show 90% confidence bounds.

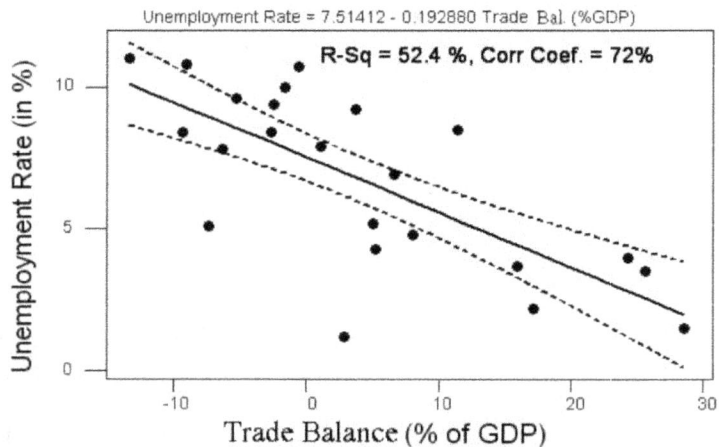

Figure 7-3 Regression analysis of Table 7-1 between Column 2, the Unemployment rate and Column 4, the Trade Deficit (%GDP) with two outliers removed. Dotted lines show 90% confidence bounds.

8

TRADE DEFICIT SUPPORTS SEPARATION OF WEALTH

The underlying economic theory of free trade agreements is that of "comparative advantage. "The theory of comparative advantage postulates that in a free marketplace, each country/area will ultimately specialize in that activity where it has comparative advantage (i.e. natural resources, skilled artisans, agriculture-friendly weather, etc.). The result should be that all parties to the pact will increase their income."[176]

However, the increases in income can be narrowed down to a reduced number of individuals. "The theory refers only to aggregate wealth and says nothing about the distribution of wealth. In fact there may be significant losers, in particular among the recently protected industries which have a comparative disadvantage. The proponents of free trade can, however, retort that the gains of the gainers exceed the losses of the losers."[177]

Thus free trade in many ways supports separation of wealth. This separation of U.S. wealth includes <u>money going to foreigners</u>. We now have to worry that the wealthy people that control U.S. dollars do not even live in America! Less money here will create poverty issues (as well as poor velocity of money[178]). We have demonstrated this in Chapter 5. We now present more data on this issue.

---

[176] http://usliberals.about.com/od/theeconomyjobs/i/FreeTradeAgmts.htm
[177] http://en.wikipedia.org/wiki/Free_trade_area
[178] http://en.wikipedia.org/wiki/Velocity_of_money

8.1 Separation of Wealth 1980-2008

We will focus on the years between 1980 and 2008. We briefly review a strong piece of evidence that was presented in Section 3.1.2 from an MIT Study[179] on the Trade Deficit Effects

"...increased exposure of local labor markets to Chinese imports leads to higher unemployment, lower labor force participation, and reduced wages. The employment reduction is concentrated in manufacturing, and explains one third of the aggregate decline in U.S. manufacturing employment between 1990 and 2007. Wage declines occur in the broader local labor market, however, and are most pronounced outside of manufacturing. Growing import exposure spurs a substantial increase in transfer payments to individuals and households in the form of unemployment insurance benefits, disability benefits, income support payments, and in-kind medical benefits.

The decline of product manufacturing in the U.S. with cheaper labor overseas results in higher profits for fewer people, and this corresponds to lower labor force participation and reduced wages. This is a key result with the effect related to separation of wealth. It represents lost opportunities for many Americans.

Remark 8.1: "...In the United States, wealth is highly concentrated in relatively few hands. As of 2007, the top 1% of households (the upper class) owned 34.6% of all privately held wealth, and the next 19% (the managerial, professional, and small business stratum) had 50.5%, which means that just 20% of the people owned a remarkable 85%, leaving only 15% of the wealth for the bottom 80% (wage and salary workers)...."[180]

To look at separation of wealth due to the trade deficit, we will study the period from 1980 to 2008, as much of the relevant statistics are available for this period. The figure below provides an overview of the separation of wealth that has occurred in the U.S. since 1980. This graph plots IRS data of ***Adjusted Gross Income*** (AGI)[181] as a percent of the total AGI earned by each percentage group. Here we focus on the bottom 50% who's AGI had declined from 17.7% to 12.7% from 1980 to 2008, a decline of about 5%. This occurred while the top 1%, 5% and 10% AGI have increased 11.5%, 13.7% and 13.6% respectively over this time period.

---

[179]D. Autor, D. Dorn, G. Hanson, The China Syndrome: Local Labor Market Effects of Import Competition in the United States http://econ-www.mit.edu/files/6613

[180] http://sociology.ucsc.edu/whorulesamerica/power/wealth.html

[181] www.taxfoundation.org/news/show/250.html

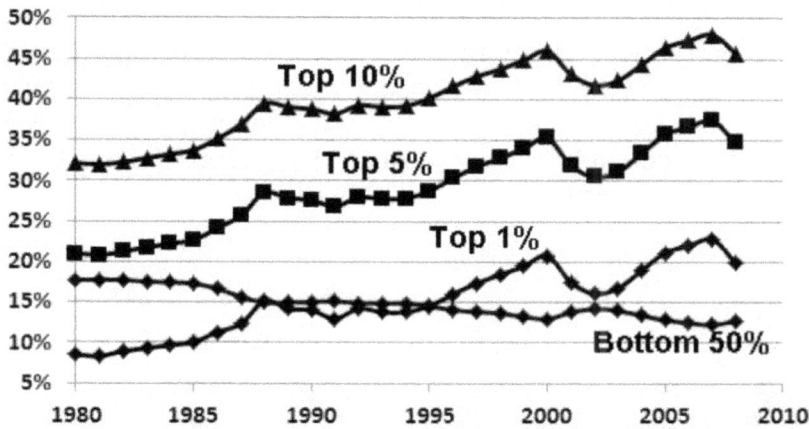

Figure 8-1 Adjusted gross income percent of total AGI earned by each percentage group showing the decline of bottom 50%.

In order to see the separation, we plot it as a percent change compared to the bottom 50%. The next graph looks at the top 1% and top 50% both relative to the separation from the **bottom** 50% in Figure 8-1. For example over this time period from 1980 to 2008, the top 1% increased in AGI by 11.5% while the bottom 50% decreased by 5% providing a total separation of 16.5% by 2008. This is the final 2008 data point shown on the below graph. Here we see comparison for the Top 1% separation of wealth to the Bottom 50% (top line).

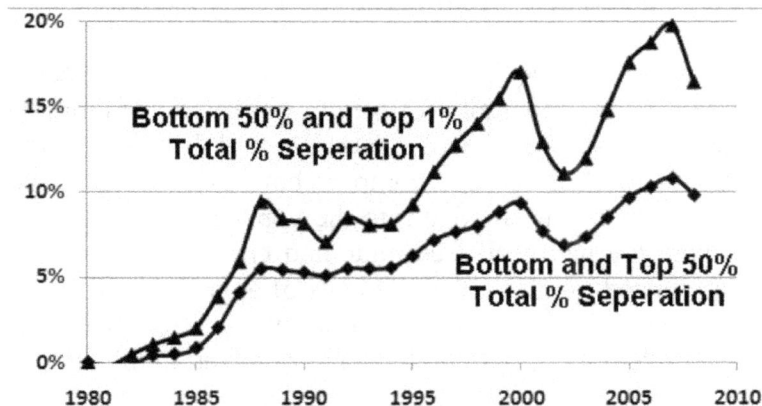

Figure 8-2 Separation of wealth of the bottom 50% compared to top 1% (top line) and compared to top 50% (bottom line) [182]
As well there is a comparison of the top 50% separation of wealth to the bottom 50%

---

[182] www.taxfoundation.org/news/show/250.html

(lower line).

At this point we start to look at the trade deficit and see how it may have affected separation of wealth. The figure below shows the trade deficit data[183] by year in this time period from 1980 to 2008. Actually, while the trade deficit started in 1971, almost the entire significant U.S. deficit has occurred since 1980. Therefore this is a very relevant time series in U.S. trading history.

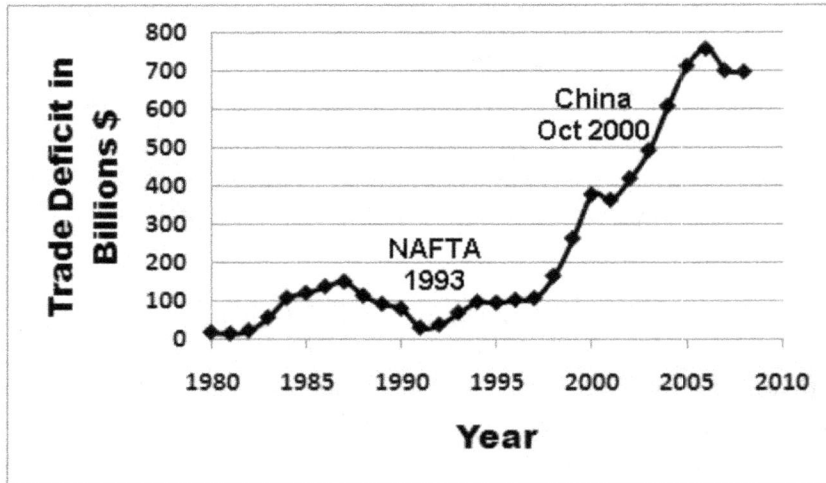

Figure 8-3 U.S. yearly trade deficit from 1980 to 2008

8.2 Exhibit A-5 Separation of Wealth and the Trade Deficit

Now we would like to compare the trends in the time series of trade deficits in Figure 8-3 and compare it to the separation of wealth observed in Figure 8-2 over this time period. To do so we must normalize the data. We will do this by normalizing to 100% of the 2008 value in each graph and compare both trend lines to see how they compare. In Figure 8-2 we will normalize it to the upper line (Top 1% and Bottom 50%). Recall that we note the theory of free trade and comparative advantage can increase the income to a reduced number of individuals of aggregate wealth and poor distribution of wealth. Thus it is appropriate to look at the Top 1% and Bottom 50% and compare it to the trade deficit, with both data normalized in this time period.

The results are displayed in the figure below. We note a strong similar time series for each normalized data group. Here we have two data sets having a time series that trend up in a similar manner. The evidence is not totally conclusive that the trade deficit is

---

[183] www.census.gov/foreign-trade/statistics/historical/gands.pdf

the direct cause for the separation of wealth observed by Figure 8-2 trend lines but does provide important insight in light of the MIT study. Certainly the evidence is enough to merit further study and question the logic to promoting a trade policy that is likely increasing separation of wealth in the United States.

Figure 8-4 Normalized to 2008, the Trade Deficit line compared to Separation of wealth line of the Top 1% and Bottom 50%

We briefly remind the reader that even rich Americans will at some point start to decrease in population as more and more money ends up in the hands of foreign controlled assets as described in Chapter 5. Here we have stated that the trade deficit enables foreign ownership of U.S. reinvestment dollars.

8.3 The Role of the Wealthy in Causing the National Debt
Every tax loophole is a burden to the general population. The wealthy created these loopholes (as we have discussed in Chapter 3) playing a large role in creating the U.S. national debt crisis and they should now pay the price.

There are myths perpetuated every year that 1) the wealthy pay their fair share of the taxes and their taxes should not be increased, and 2) that the wealthy cannot pay off the national debt though tax increases.

The reason we present information on this, while it may seem off the topic of the trade deficit, is that we have connected the trade deficit to both separation of wealth and to increase in the national debt. It is important for the reader to realize that if the non-wealthy end up paying off the national debt through losses of entitlements like

Medicare, the trade deficit is partly responsible. Furthermore, if the non-wealthy end up paying for the national debt problem, it will further increase separation of wealth.

8.3.1 The Myth that the Wealthy Pay Their Fair Share

Given the fact that the under-taxed wealthy could pay off the national debt in 12 years, which we will show, with a higher tax rate, why should anyone give up their entitlements for them (such as Medicare)?

There is a wealth of information that shows individuals in recent years are making extraordinarily increasing yearly incomes, many times greater than the current upper tax bracket of about $270,000. In one case **a hedge-fund manager John Paulson made $3.7 billion in 2007**[184] (by apparently betting on the U.S. housing crisis), with other hedge fund managers not far behind him in billion dollar yearly salaries. This individual actually paid substantially less than his 35% bracket, a reported 15% - the same tax as someone making approximately $34,000. This is another loophole that hedge fund managers lobbied to obtain[185]. John Paulson has also been accused of starting the housing crisis[186] with marketing rumors that caused panic, resulting in failing bank mortgage-back securities that he bet against. Congress has done nothing to fix such issues or investigate this accusation.

Note that dividing his earnings, $3.7 billion by $270,000 (top level tax bracket) results in a factor of 9,920 times larger than the upper tax income bracket! This is a disturbing reality prompting a serious look at the U.S. tax structure.

If we look at the upper tax brackets and plot it versus income and add the $3.7 billion that was made by Paulson, we immediately see the problem in Figure 8-5.

The irregular line more clearly illustrates how unfair the wealthy taxes can be. The logical increase has been added using a dotted line. The figure shows our tax structure clearly is uneven and favors the upper income individuals since it is not extended. That is, prior to 35% the more money a person makes the higher his tax bracket, except after $270,000. The question is, why does it stop there? It should continue to be consistent and fair. This indicates that a disproportionate tax is removed at the lower end compared to the upper income tax bracket (i.e. it is unequal at the upper

---

[184] www.earthtimes.org/articles/show/199378,hedge-fund-manager-paulson-earns-37-billion.html
[185] Tax breaks for billionaires: Loophole for hedge fund managers costs billions in tax revenue, Randall Dodd July 24, 2007, http://www.epi.org/publications/entry/pm120/
[186] The Man Who Made Too Much, G.Weiss, Jan 07 2009
www.portfolio.com/executives/features/2009/01/07/John-Paulson-Profits-in-Downturn

and lower ends). The upper level should be equally weighted as shown by the dotted line.

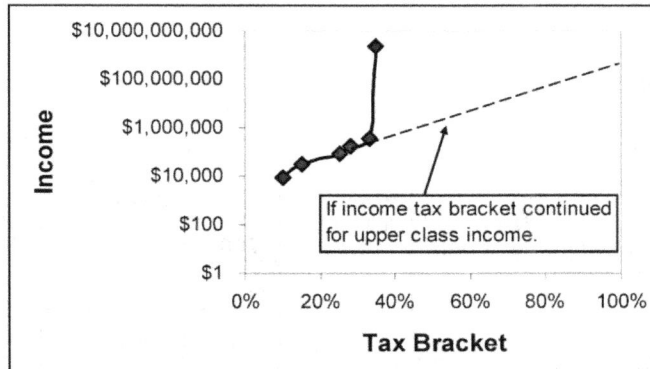

Figure 8-5 2009 tax bracket versus upper income level with dashed line showing the logical continuation of the bracket

Furthermore, the wealthy in the 35% bracket find multiple loopholes and do not even pay close to this bracket requirement. The table below provides the information on what they paid, around 23%, in 2008 compared to their bracket.

Table 8-1 Average Tax Rate Actually Paid in 2008 in the 33 or 35% Bracket [187]

Wealthy Top Percent	Number of Returns with Positive AGI	Group's Share of Income Taxes	Minimum Income	Bracket	Average Tax Rate
Top 0.1%	140,000	18.47%	$1,803,585	35%	**22.7%**
Top 1%	1,400,000	38.02%	$380,354	35%	**23.3%**
Top 5%	7,000,000	58.72	$159,619	28%	20.7

8.4 Wealthy Can Pay Off the National Debt – They Helped Create it and Should

We can do a simple calculation to show that the wealthy top 1% could pay off the national debt in 12 years if we collected a tax of 70% on their income.

There is a strong precedent for a higher income tax rate. In fact, the income tax during World War II reached 94%.

---

[187] www.taxfoundation.org/news/show/250.html

Remark 8.2: "The rate had reached 94% during World War II on income over $200,000 (approx. $2.5 million in today's dollars). It dropped down to 91% in 1946 and remained there until the Kennedy tax cuts in 1962-64. Brackets weren't inflation adjusted back then; they had reached $1.4 million in today's dollars."[188]

Let's review a snapshot of the tax revenues collected in years 2007 and 2009 in the below table.

Table 8-2 Overview of Tax Revenues Collected 2007, 2009[189]

Type of Return	Number of Returns	Gross Collected in Millions $ 2009	Percent 2009	Gross Collected in Millions $ 2007	Percent 2007
Individual income tax	144,103,375	1,175,422	50.4%	1,236,259	49.1%
Corporation income tax	2,475,785	225,482	9.7%	380925	15.1%
Employment taxes	30,223,289	858,164	36.8%	814819	32.4%
Excise taxes	809,461	46,632	2.0%	57,990	0.1%
Gift tax	245,262	3,094	0.1%	1970	2.3%
Estate tax	47,320	21,583	0.9%	26,717	1.1%
Total Revenues Collected		**2,330,377**		**2,518,680**	

Now let's do a back-of-the-paper type estimate to show that the under-taxed top 1% could pay off the National debt if they paid their fair share.

Here is the simple calculation that any high school student could do.
1) The total average income tax revenue collected in Table 8-2 is about $1.2 trillion each year.
2) The wealthy top 1% pay about 38% of this (see Table 8-2) which comes to $0.46 trillion.
3) However the wealthy top 1% only pays taxes at a rate of about 23%. Most of them are severely under-taxed. We mentioned earlier how hedge fund manager, John Paulson paid only a 15% tax on $3.7 billion he made.
4) If we triple the wealthy tax from 23% collected to 69% collected that would be an

Extra= $0.92 trillion

The second group that has helped to cause the national deficit problem is corporations who have lobbied for tax breaks. Corporations now pay less than 10% of all IRS revenue collected as shown in Table 8-2! If trade were balanced, as it should be,

---

[188] www.taxfoundation.org/blog/show/23697.html
[189] http://www.irs.gov/taxstats/article/0,,id=102886,00.html

corporations would be more prone to paying their fair share (i.e., tax breaks are under the premise that they need to be globally competitive and balanced trade would help). They would also have to hire more American workers with balanced trade. The current corporate tax situation is certainly unfair to American workers. If the corporate rate were to double this would collect another

Extra 0.23 trillion (see Table 8-2)

(see Table 8-2). This brings the total extra tax revenues that could be collected from the wealthy top 1% and corporations to a total

Extra Tax Revenues=$1.15 trillion

From section 4.4, we estimated that the trade deficit adds about $60 billion to $180 billion each year to the national debt due to unbalance trade. If we take the average of these values we would pick up another $0.12 trillion by balancing trade.

Then the total would be
Extra tax revenues collected = $1.27 trillion.

Using this figure, the current $14 trillion national debt could be paid off in about 11 years.

Given these facts why would the population of citizens who are not in the top 1% category (comprising 99% of the U.S. population) want to lose their entitlements (such as Medicare) if the wealthy top 1% could mostly pay off the national debt in 11 years?

8.5 Separation of Wealth Needs to be Settled in a Court of Law

The reality is, congress now keeps passing tax loop holes for the rich. This is taking dollars from every non wealthy American who ends up having the burden to make up for these tax losses. This is an unjust use of public allocation of monies and should be against the law. Since congress will not fix this, we recommend taking this matter to court. We have provided evidence by Citizens for Tax Justice that there is little being done and these loop holes are out of control. There is more than enough evidence. With a stalemate congress, separation of wealth taxation issues should be brought to a court of law to force legislation for fair taxation.

9

BALANCED TRADE – WHY IT IS FAR SUPERIOR TO FREE TRADE & HOW IT IS IMPLEMENTED

The solution proposed in this book is to have an effective balanced trade policy. The only way to accomplish this is with proper political economic tools to help congress do proper problem solving. These are proposed in Chapter 11. Balanced trade is a simple concept which says that a country should import only as much as it exports so that trade and money flows are balanced. The reader should note that there is no WTO agreement that says the U.S. cannot seek to balance its trade. Here we would like to see the U.S. trade deficit, over a reasonable adjustment time period, start to be limited and slowly be reduced to almost zero. If we can send a man to the moon, we surely can find a way to balance trade.

9.1 Why is Balanced Trade Far Superior to Free Trade?

The reader is now in a position to understand why balanced trade is far superior to free trade. There is now ample data to show that free trade does not work in the real world. Economic greed runs rampant and this cannot be stopped without balanced trade. The table below provides a direct comparison between the two, presenting the basic reasons. We note that most of these reasons have a root cause problem related to greed issues. However, there are likely more effects on our economy that can be compared. The issues presented in the table below have been well discussed in this book and now serve somewhat as a summary. We will point out two important points. First free trade puts America's economy at risk because of the large yearly trade deficits. It is similar to an aging nuclear reactor that will explode and ruin America's economy in time due to foreign ownership increases. There is no way around this with large annual trade deficits that keep transferring annually about $0.6 trillion U.S. dollars to foreigners. The effect of foreign ownership is well discussed in this book. The key draw backs include American businesses and land being sold to foreigners. This adds up to losing control of the U.S. As well, data has shown that foreign controlled domestic corporations cause terrible U.S. job growth (see Chapter 5).

Table 9-1 Comparison Between Free Trade and Balanced Trade

Effect on America	Free Trade with Large Trade Deficits	Balanced Trade Minimizing Trade Deficits
Eliminates the Trade Deficit	No	Yes
Encourages foreign ownership of U.S. businesses and U.S. property.	Yes	No - stops giving foreigners trade deficit dollars used to purchase U.S. assets.
Encourages Currency Manipulation	Yes	No – would stop it.
Encourages Foreign Cheating	Yes	No –more controllable
Encourages Trade Wars	Yes	No – real comparative advantages would be optimized
Allows America's Comparative Advantage to be Optimization	No	Yes – U.S. industries have time to optimize before forced to manufac. Overseas.
Minimizes Inflation	Yes	To some extent
Encourages U.S. Manufacturing	No	Yes – More products forced to be made domestically.
Stifles Job Growth	Yes	No – more manufacturing will be required in U.S.
Creates Added National Debt	Yes	No
Help Balance the National Debt	No	Yes – jobs = revenues
Reduces Offshoring, Outsourcing and Tax Loopholes	No – Opposite	Yes – balance trade will bring back lots of manufacturing.
Encourages Greed Problems	Yes	No – much reduced
Encourages Separation of Wealth	Yes	No – more manufacturing, more jobs and opportunities.
Produces foreign ownership	Yes	No unequal foreign ownership
Puts the U.S. Economy at High Risk of Collapse	Yes	No

Second, we believe that balanced trade outshines free trade in the area of comparative advantage! We argue this for multiple reasons. However, the two main reasons are that:

- Balanced trade fights greed where free trade encourages it. Thus balanced trade has a built in greed protection that free trade does not. Free trade actually creates a comparative disadvantage for U.S. companies.

- Free trade exploits low wage earning countries and does not give a chance for high wage earning countries to optimize their own comparative advantage. For example, the steel industry in the U.S. cannot and should not be competing with a wealthy Chinese government that subsidizes and dumps products in the U.S to cripple this industry. The steel industry can likely compete on a level playing field if they are kept strong and have time to optimize their business model. This is true of solar panels: China's government (not its industries) has put U.S. manufacturers out of business through over-subsidizing to gain control of this business (see Chapter 6).

9.2 How it is implemented

As we mentioned in the beginning of this chapter, the only real way to implement any effective economic policy including balancing trade is by using proper political economic problem solving tools such as what we propose in Chapter 11. There are many ideas to start with when we do problem solving on this political economic issue. In general:

Remark 9.1: "A country can balance its trade either on a trading partner basis in which total money flows between two countries are equalized, or it can balance the overall trade and money flows so that a trade deficit with one country is balanced by a trade surplus with another country."[190]

Warren Buffett had an excellent suggestion that we recommend under reasonable modifications[191]:

Remark 9.2: "Balanced trade has been advocated by Warren Buffett, who suggested a system of "Import Certificates" (ICs) – exporters would receive $1 of ICs for each $1 of goods they exported, and importers would be required to present $1 of ICs for every $1 of goods they import. This would limit the value of imports to at most the value of exports (and presumably exactly the value of imports, assuming no leakage), and create a market of exporters to sell ICs to importers, effectively subsidizing exporters and taxing importers."

Remark 9.3: In the United States, Buffett's idea was first introduced legislatively in the *Balanced Trade Restoration Act of 2006*. The proposed legislation was

---

[190] McKeever, Sr, Michael (1996). *Balanced Trade: Toward the Future of Economics*. McKeever Institute of Economic Policy Analysis. http://www.mkeever.com/essay.html. Retrieved 2008-04-16.
[191] http://en.wikipedia.org/wiki/Balanced_trade

sponsored by Senators Byron Dorgan (ND) and Russell Feingold (WI), two Democrats in the United States Senate. The bill was never voted on. Since then there has been no action on the bill.

9.3 The Myth of the Smoot-Hawley Tariff Act and Resistance to Balancing Trade

Some economists claim that trade cannot be balanced using import tariffs that could start a trade war based on superficial arguments surrounding a Hawley-Smoot Tariff Act of 1930 that has been cited as causing an economic downturn. However there are numerous articles[192,193] that such claims are a total myth. While we will not list these, we will mention one key point that is often overlooked. At the time of this tariff, America had a trade surplus. This is important since the U.S. at the time was more of a seller than a customer as it is now. There is in fact no historical detrimental evidence to suggest that balancing trade with tariffs during a time of a trade deficit can significantly impact an economy.

---

[192] www.votefordavea.com/resource/smoot-hawley-myth
[193] www.freerepublic.com/focus/f-news/2178473/posts

10

WHAT IS WRONG WITH POLITICAL ECONOMICS?
- THE GAP -

W̲e note that 90% of economists are free trade advocates, yet none of them can defend the U.S. trade deficit. What does this say about economists who appear to accept the good with the very bad? It means that economics itself is an incomplete science having a gap that is unable to deal with the real world "greed" factors. In this chapter, we explain the need for an Office of Reliability and Quality Economics.

The key gap that exist is in our *"political economy."* The term political economy means not only an interaction between economists and government but their ability to do proper problem solving and protect policies against the greed factor. The gap between politicians and economists is extremely wide. Politicians are looking for votes, economists are schooled in ideology, and this creates huge problems. Politicians need some political economic tools, but they have none. Economists need methods to incorporate such factors as greed and long-term reliability issues into economic policy.

U.S. policies continue to be generated with severe under-design, poor tracking, and an inability to be changed once they are signed into law. Therefore, if the policy has a fault, it cannot evolve and improve without complex debate, lobbyist interference, and the full voting process.

In this chapter we look at how industry has dealt with real-world issues and filled their gap, and we explain how their methods should and could be adopted for government to fill this gap proposing the need for an Office of Reliability and Quality economics. This would be a bipartisan solution that would not change our method of government. Before the 1950s, companies recognized their gap and developed a science to bridge such problems so that products like automobiles and airplanes could be dependable in the real world. Similar to the greed factor, industry has to deal with their harsh environments like difficult weather conditions and customer abuse on products. Consumers would not tolerate under-designed automobiles or airplanes for example. Therefore, industry developed another science to make up for their engineer design short falls as they tracked field issues and found problems that needed fixing. Today, the mature disciplines that supplements designers are the sciences of reliability and quality engineering. These engineers work with design engineers, management, and marketing. These engineers are focused in industry on problem solving with tools that are used to help the engineering design team and management improve products. Such tools are designed to help constantly ask questions like: How can we improve customer satisfaction? What could go wrong with the design? How could the car fail? What are the potential failure modes and root causes? How can we test it to check for any failure modes and assure it operates as needed? Then they would work with the design team to seek corrective action for the root cause problems.

This was their gap that is now filled everyday in industry by reliability and quality engineers. They work with the design team so that the design works in the real world. Political Economics has this serious gap that unlike industry has not been filled; this gap could be filled similarly with what we call reliability economics. This science was introduced in his prior book[194]. Here we have suggested that an office of reliability and quality economics be developed as a bipartisan solution to the political economy. For example, one key tool that is used in almost every industry today that could easily be adopted by a bipartisan committee studying a political economic problem is called Failure Modes Effects Analysis (FMEA). This is a method where teams come together to do problem solving in a structured way.

10.1 Reliability Economics – The Gap
We have detailed the use of the science of reliability in his prior book that includes a full chapter on Reliability Economics and the need for an Office of Reliability and Quality Economics. The award-winning book demonstrates its many uses. Congress people propose solutions to fix one thing and cause failure elsewhere. They jump to solutions without understanding root causes. They comprise mostly of lawyers who need political economic tools. They currently have very little tools available to do

---

[194] The Truth of the Modern Recession, Root Causes & Reliable Solutions, Introducing Reliability Economics, www.amazon.com/Truth-Modern-Recession-Reliable-Solutions/dp/0615315291

proper problem solving and work in a corner expecting others to agree with their proposed solutions.

Reliability science has been used successfully by industry for years in every engineering discipline from aircraft to automotive design. Why not economics? Due to this science, industry's products over the last 100 years have increased in safety, quality and reliability while real world economics has decreased in safety and quality and are very unreliable.

To make this clear, Table 10-1 demonstrates some of the achievements of reliability science since 1950 and we will compare this to Economics since 1950.

Table 10-1 Industry Accomplishments with Reliability Science

System	Reliability Achievements Over Time 1950
Automotive 1956 (FORD)	6 months or 6,000 Miles
Automotive 1982 (FORD	2 Years of 24,000 Miles
Automotive 1999 (Hyundai)	5 Years or 60,000 Miles
Aircraft (1950)	6 Fatal Failures out of 2,484,000 =0.000242%
Aircraft (1997)	3 Fatal Failures out of 8,157,000 =0.000037%
Space Shuttle	2 Failures of 128 = 1.5% (Challenger, Columbia)

We contrast Table 10-1 to the progress of macroeconomics in the U.S. without reliability and quality oversight in Table 10-2.

Table 10-2 Economy Without Reliability Science

Economic Policy	Approximately Last 10 Years
National Debt	More Than Doubled ($14 Trillion)
Manufacturing Job Losses -	Up 40%
Trade Deficit – (2000 China enters U.S. free trade)	Tripled ($7.5 Trillion since 1971)
Separation of Wealth	Increases 1% per Year (Increase 28%, 1980-2007)
Unemployment	Doubled

Repeal Glass-Steagall act of 1933 (1999-Present)	733 Banks Bailed Out 229 Bank Failures and related are: Collapse Lehman Brother, Bear Stearns Debacle
Lobbyist Influences:	Increased
Business Failure Rate	Increased
Housing Failure Rate	Increased

You might look at Table 10-2 and wonder how one can blame a macroeconomic gap on many of these failing policies. Shouldn't we blame our politicians? The answer is NO. We must blame the gap on failure of proper political economic oversight. Industry had no small task in making their improvements over time against its environment. If we are to survive, we need proper oversight. This can only be accomplished with a bipartisan solution of reliability macroeconomics. Why is it a bipartisan solution? Mainly because we foresee that every policy could and should at some point go through the same problem solving methods prior to being voted on with a bipartisan committee headed by an Office of Quality and Reliability economists. A reliability economist would not make or propose the policies, just as they do not do the design in industry. However, they would help investigate and question the short falls of potential policies with interested members of a bipartisan congressional team. How much easier would it be to pass a piece of legislation that has had a bipartisan committee that has done its problem solving up front and designed its policies correctly protecting against the greed factor.

Reliability has enabled industry to improve poor designs. Free trade's design is still living in the dark ages. We can do better than that. We do not have to put up with the numerous failure modes of free trade.

The failure modes of free trade are numerous and all require corrective action. These failure modes that we have discussed include:

1) Job outsourcing, 2) Manufacturing failure & decline, 3) U.S. corporation failures, 4) Lost tax revenue due to layoffs and trade deficit, 5) Narrow focus on U.S. wealth and more…

These failure modes lead to the following effects:

1) Increase in unemployment, 2) Foreign-dominated businesses, 3) Spending cutbacks or increases in national debt, 4) Increase in foreign U.S. business ownership

and debt to foreigners, 5) Increases in separation of wealth, 6) Product counterfeiting, 7) Product dumping … etc

The failure modes need to be studied and the root causes identified. The root causes include:

Cheaper labor, foreign subsidies, foreign currency manipulation, violation of free trade policy, lack of government oversight, job outsourcing, business failures due to foreign competition, trade deficit, high- versus low-wage economies, lack of non–trade war protectionism measures.

Potential corrective actions would include addressing issues with WTO. Penalize foreign imports for violations, class action law suits, import certificates (see Warren Buffett plan), scalable tariff, VAT tax, and other ways to help balance trade.

This is the failure of political macroeconomics. They have no reliability science like industry. Industry lives in the real world. Yet our government has no Office of Reliability and Quality economics team. How can America, with so much at stake, defend policies with built-in failure modes and so many known effects and greed factors that are not guarded against and that lead to the need corrective actions? Instead of putting out fires in government, why not prevent them in the first place? A reliability team would start by seeking to do problem solving with bipartisan members of Congress helping to find ways to balancing trade and guarding against unwanted real-world greed effects. Reliability economists would be a trained team to specifically look at the root causes of failure modes and work with Congress in this bipartisan manner for solutions.

Right now, without reliability economics filling the gap, economists are highly dangerous people. They are designers without any checks or balances. They make recommendations to politicians who trust their expertise. Would you board an aircraft knowing that no reliability engineer had spent time overseeing the design? This is what Congress does every day. Many politicians and citizens have read books by famous economists who are trained professional and have studied all aspects of free trade. Yet they are not skilled in the science of reliability and have no such mindset. Let's look at such a book by one of the most renowned authors on the subject of free trade from a reliability perspective.

In the next section, we provide "reliability" critiques on famous economists to illustrate the dangerous nature of their approach that includes disregard for future reliability impacts to the economy.

10.2 Economic Experts Who Many Trust Miss the Mark

You might ask, "Don't America's finest political economists understand intuitively reliability economics?" Here we provide examples that many of our economists that we trust really do not understand the principles of problem solving in order to achieve a reliable economy.

10.2.1 "Free Trade Under Fire" is Irresponsibly Written – Book Review
by Dr. Alec Feinberg on October 18, 2010

Free Trade Under Fire written by Douglas Irwin, Prof. of Economics at Dartmouth College, is an irresponsible biased work and a deterrent to responsible balanced trade reform. First and foremost, the title is incorrect; it is not Free Trade that is under fire by trade reformists[195,196] rather its fundamental failure mode, the Trade Deficit, and its consequences. In the U.S. you cannot have Free Trade without a Trade Deficit. Therefore, as a reader, I was disappointed that Douglas does not address the issue of how large yearly trade deficits could impact the U.S. economy's reliability over time. Fundamental Economics indicates and common sense indicates that no country can long sustain large yearly trade deficits without putting its economy at risk[197].

Free Trade advocates like Irwin seem to disregard key facts such as 1) these large trade deficits have now substantially increased the national debt due to constant tax losses primarily from job losses, outsourcing, and offshoring[198,199,200] (See Chapter 3 and 4). Such constant tax losses add to the U.S. debt burdening our citizens. This is a huge U.S. reverse tariff. Yet Irwin and others in his position oppose any tariffs. So left unanswered is this fact that, not only do we have massive job losses, but ordinary citizens are forced to subsidize free trade's failures paying for these layoffs

---

[195] Trade Reform Organizations all fighting to reduce the trade deficit:
www.CitizensForEqualTrade.org, http://www.americaneconomicalert.com,
http://www.prosperousamerica.org/, www.citizenstrade.org
[196] Fletcher, Ian. "Free Trade Doesn't Work", 2010
[197] Biggest Threat to America's Future --The U.S. Trade Deficit,
http://www.tradereform.org/2010/08/biggest-threat-to-americas-future-the-u-s-free-trade-deficit/,
http://economyincrisis.org/content/biggest-threat-americas-future-us-free-trade-deficit-0
[198] Trade Deficit's Reverse Tariff Increased the U.S. National Debt – an 84% Correlation!
http://economyincrisis.org/content/trade-deficit%E2%80%99s-reverse-tariff-increased-us-national-debt-%E2%80%93-84-correlation-0
[199] Reverse Tariff - Economic Crisis Due to Free Trade's Flaw (Aug. 2, 2010)
http://economyincrisis.org/content/reverse-tariff-economic-crisis-due-free-trades-flaw
[200] Feinberg, Alec. The Truth of the Modern Recession, Root Causes and Reliable Solutions, Introducing Reliability Economics. WE-Economy Press, 2009

through the huge tax losses! 2) He also overlooks the fact that foreigners now own between roughly 23% of all U.S. businesses but only employ about 3.7% of the workforce (see prior chapters). 3) This is the result of the enormous cumulative U.S. trade deficit where foreigners now own $8.5 trillion more of us than we do of them, another key fact he chooses not to discuss. 4) Foreign business in the U.S. also ends up paying less tax which is ignored. 5) We also note that contrary to his original unemployment thesis, statistical data now available shows that countries with higher trade deficits tend to have higher unemployment[201] (see Chapter 7). 6) Overlooked is the unreliability of Free Trade. Citizens have only one life to live; they do not wish to constantly have to start over to be retrained for new jobs. 7) As well, unemployment government sponsored education programs add to the national debt. 8) Finally, Free Traders like Irwin do not perform any fundamental root cause analysis, which is basic to Reliability Economics[202] (see Chapter 10).

I have spoken to him recently on the radio[203] about the trade deficit and he suggests that Americans should save more. This in my modest opinion is not a practical answer to what America's number one problem is and what his book should be about. The key difference between Irwin Douglas and his admired Adam Smith and David Ricardo, free trade originators, is that Dr. Douglas now has mounds of modern data that should be used to see how these large cumulative U.S. trade deficits are taking their toll on the reliability of the U.S. economy. Like a piece of metal that is bent back and forth, the cumulative damage will eventually show up and cause the metal to break. The economy is interrelated; Dr. Douglas and others like him disregard these long term trade deficit consequences such as increases in the national debt, greater separation of wealth, foreign ownership, America for sale, mortgage delinquencies related to outsourced job losses, etc.. All these issues are left behind apparently choosing ideology over data.

Another issue is that they always refer to Smoot-Hawley's 1930 tariff failure which he does not point out was implemented at a time when the U.S. had a trade surplus Tariffs are known to be most effective to balance trade when a country has some clout as a valued customer. He also feels that the Smoot-Hawley Act was somewhat of a contributor to the Great Depression even though most economists claim this is a myth[204]. Eager to persuade the reader, this and other comments are not put into

---

[201] Trade Deficit Countries Have Higher Unemployment-Balanced Trade is Needed, http://economyincrisis.org/content/trade-deficit-countries-have-higher-unemployment-rates--balanced-trade-needed
[202] Feinberg, Alec. The Truth of the Modern Recession, Root Causes and Reliable Solutions, Introducing Reliability Economics. WE-Economy Press, 2009
[203] Irwin Douglas, Guest Speaker on Bob Brinker, Money Talk, 2010.
[204] Fletcher, Ian. "Free Trade Doesn't Work", 2010

proper perspective. Still, if we agree, it does not answer the question ... how to get rid of these enormous yearly trade deficits.

And what protects Americans now against cheating? WTO safeguards are not as effective as he suggests. Free trade policy actually encourages foreigners to cheat as every country wants to export America to death. Contrary to free trade theory, America is at a "Comparative Disadvantage" (see Chapter 11). Well known is unethical trade deficit problems related to: Currency Manipulation, Excessive Job Outsourcing, Foreign Product Subsidies, Non tariff Trade Barriers, Lack of Intellectual Prop-Property Rights Protection, and Product Counterfeiting. Free traders know this but seems to perpetuate the WTO as the best we can do rather than own up to the failure of "Comparative Advantage." A good trade policy should protect American citizens. I was disappointed that he did not step outside the box and even consider the benefits of something like a balanced trade policy[205]. Balanced Trade would of course eliminate the trade deficit, not violate WTO policy, and would discourage cheating.

Dr. Douglas misses the boat on exploring the full cumulative reliability effects of the now $8.5 trillion U.S trade deficit. I doubt that even Adam Smith or David Ricardo ever really intended their theories would properly apply in the extreme case of today's U.S. massive trade deficits, (with 59% going to communist China in 2009)..

You might ask, could a panel of experts fix our economy? The following article demonstrates that reliability economists are not the same as economist.

10.2.2 How to Fix the Economy, Experts Ignore the U.S. Trade Deficit
by Dr. Alec Feinberg on December 26, 2010

On September 7th, 2010, a highly distinguished Bloomberg Business week panel of experts discussed how to fix the U.S. economy[206]. These out-of-touch experts failed to discuss what most Americans know the key problem is, the U.S. $8 Trillion Trade Deficit which causes outsourcing and off-shoring job losses. In addition, due to con-

---

[205] Proposed Balance of Trade Restoration Act 2006, http://en.wikipedia.org/wiki/Balanced_trade

[206] www.businessweek.com/magazine/content/10_39/b4196054741296.htm, On September 7, Bloomberg Businessweek brought together four top economists to discuss, *How to fix the American Economy*. Panel consisted of Yale University professor Robert J. Shiller, author of *Irrational Exuberance*; Peter R. Orszag, who recently stepped down as director of President Obama's Office of Management & Budget; financial consultant and former Salomon Brothers Managing Director Henry Kaufman; and Professor Charles W. Calomiris, who is the Henry Kaufman Professor of Financial Institutions at Columbia University. Pimco Managing Director William H. Gross, who runs the world's biggest bond fund, joined the group by telephone

stant trade deficit, job losses equate to serious loss of tax revenues putting the U.S. in more debt threatening our future. This goes to show how out-of-touch with reality distinguished experts can be in the U.S.A.

We need experts who not only can think outside the box but can relate to the millions of Americans who can't find work. For example, they at least could have acknowledged the trade deficit and how it has affected the economy. They might look at some logical proposals such as The Balance of Trade Restoration Act of 2006[207] which would not violate the WTO. America's trade deficit is nearly 10 times worse than any other trade deficit country! Pretending that China's currency manipulation will be solved and cure our trade deficit problems is another fantasy economists wrapped up in "free trade" ideology have, rather than understanding that global economic greed can't be stopped without a proper trade policy.

We need a trade policy that stops cheating, such as a balance of trade proposal that will help bring back U.S. manufacturing jobs. Until then, the trade deficit will just keep empowering foreigners to cheat, make huge profits, and buy up American businesses with their reinvested U.S. dollars they earn. Foreigners now own between 15 to 20 percent of all U.S. businesses and only employ about 3.5 percent of the workforce[208]. American businesses and jobs are for sale and the U.S. will continue on this destructive path until U.S. economists can see the rug being pulled from under them.

---

[207] http://en.wikipedia.org/wiki/Balanced_trade
[208] Biggest Threat to America's Future --The U.S. Trade Deficit (June 14, 2010) http://economyincrisis.org/content/biggest-threat-americas-future-us-free-trade-deficit-0

11

APPENDIX 1
RELIABILITY ECONOMICS

Here we will discuss how to implement a reliability political economic corporate approach in government without interfering in the traditional legislation process. Although not interfering, a reliability corporate model could still be powerful and influential in problem solving just as it is in industry. This is not a Keynesian (government intervention) approach, but a government self-assurance program. The strong parallels between government and industry should be understood to see why this is practical. The government is like a business in that it is our largest employer. Its legislators, like in industry, are the engineers and the designers. Their product is legislation. In the model a team of quality and reliability economists would be employed to assure their product is reliable. Legislators could learn to depend on an Office of Quality and Reliability Economics as they do the Congressional Budget Office (CBO). The consumer demands customer satisfaction which means highly reliable products with good quality. In industry any good company uses a reliability and quality team that independently provides design assurance. They use a number of tools to help the design engineers (legislators) assess and find potential failure modes in the proposed product (legislation) that could prevent millions of dollars if potential failure mode(s) would otherwise escape to the consumer. In the same sense potential failure modes in a legislation bill will be highly costly. The design engineers (legislatures) do not have to implement their recommendations of the reliability assurance team in industry if they feel it will hurt the design (legislation). However, they then may put their product (legislation) at risk. The recommendations are reported, and management (Congress) becomes aware of what safeguards are built into the design (legislation) or not. This then can influence the vote on the legislation but does not interfere with the legislative voting process. The objective is to fill the ***existing reliability legislation gap*** not reviewed in the design (legislation) idea phase. In the same way that a reliability engineer does not design products, the reliability economist would not be responsible for the original legislative design. Without training, an economist would not be qualified as a reliability economist. This established reliability science should not be ignored in economics due to the high cost of failure modes. Analogous to industry, we believe in a mindset of designing it right the first time for reliability through historical understanding of the current environment, root cause investigations, and often a team approach. Classical economics may provide valuable tools but falls far short of these goals. Reliability economics provides a different set of tools such as FMEA. This tool allows for team participation. Given the difficult partisan political environment in the U.S., one of the foreseen strengths in our FMEA examples is the logical progression of root cause analysis, which is basic to problem solving, and should allow for a high level of agreement for bipartisan corrective action solutions. The key philosophy is that only through understanding root causes can solutions be found, and only when fixing failure modes can reliability growth be achieved. *People in industry can understand the need for a reliability economic corporate model in government. Politicians with no industrial experience, who have not observed the benefits, lack this foresight and understanding. This sadly presents a barrier.*

In this book we have focused on the well-known FMEA technique and applied it to the economy. However, to meet the challenge of today's economy we envision it will require developing a reliability economic team with a mindset to design-in reliability into the economy. Just as in industry, it is one thing to make a product; it is another to make it reliable – so too in the economy, each policy must have a reliability economist that is responsible to ensure it will be written to design for reliability. We anticipate that this team would perform three basic activities described in Chapter 1 (adapted from industry):[1]

- Design for reliability economics
- Reliability economic verification
- Root cause fiscal analyses

Similar to industry, these activities would be the building blocks to a sound reliability program for the economy that sits on a foundation of concurrent economic engineering. Just as economists are needed in government, so too is a Design for Reliability-Economic (DfR-E) team needed that would be responsible for these three basic activities:

1. The first reliability economic activity is to support new policy to help design for reliability. This starts with the idea phase of the policy development cycle and continues until its obsolescence. Each policy should be required to have a reliability economist assigned to the project to assure it contains a positive policy for reliability improvement by utilizing known fiscal-of-failure knowledge (discussed more below) to design out potential fiscal problems. The reliability economist would help spearhead the FMEA effort ensuring that a multi-disciplinary team made up of democrats, republicans, reliability economists, and other expert participants in the area of interest, maintain a bipartisan atmosphere with a reliability mindset. The reliability economist can use a full set of DfR-E tools that might include:

   - Fiscal of Failure Analysis
   - FMEA and Benchmarking
   - Risk Mitigation Studies
   - Economic Design Studies
   - Modeling
   - Design Rules

2. The second activity is reliability economic verification. Here verification studies and demonstration tests ensure meeting the challenges of a consumer economy. Reliability verification should take place in three phases – through a historical review of known similar data, early field data tracking with small scale testing, followed by long term maturity tracking. Reliability validation techniques can include:

Table 11-1 Reliability economic validation methods

• Economic Processes	• Reliability Screening
• Reliability Monitoring	• Design Validation
• Field Data Analysis	

3. The third activity, fiscal analysis, would be critical to a reliability economist's ability to affect the design process. This should include "Fiscal-of-Failure" analysis that is defined as understanding the nature of how and why a policy can fail when it interacts with the real economy during the design's full life cycle. This includes current CBO analysis. The reliability economist should understand the consumers' use and misuse conditions and the policy's interactions to assist the design team in working around limitations inherent in the selected design approach. This would

be a key to designing and building any future policy that will meet consumer expectations. These tools include:

Table 11-2 Reliability Economic Tools

• Design Analysis • Policy interactions • Reverse Engineering of Similar Policies	• Policy Construction Break-down • Process Analysis

Reliability economics with the three proposed major activities can support a phased economic design development cycle that in industry we call ***Stage-Gate***.

Table 11-3 Stage-Gate Reliability Economic Approach

Phase	Stage-Gate	Task	Description
1	Idea	Designing-in Reliability	Concurrent engineering approach tools such as Failure Modes and Effects Analysis (FMEA) and benchmarking to other policies. Ensure that consumer requirements are met.
2	Evaluate	Design Assessment Reliability Testing, Fiscal of Failure Analysis	Risk mitigation studies and reliability growth efforts focus on finding and fixing failure modes/ root causes, concurrent with the design process. Using the techniques of reliability growth, life testing with Test Analyze and Fix (TAAF) and others as necessary for the economic design.
3	Develop	Design Maturity Testing	Demonstrate that a design is reliably meeting the consumers' expectation. Perform statistically significant tests, usually on a small scale.
4	Transition	Screening	Ensure early design is robust. Check for infant mortality problems in the field.
5	Production (implementation)	Monitoring	Ensure continual design reliability and quality to design obsolesces.

The Stage-Gate method is shown in Table 11-1. The Stage-Gate effort would underpin economic design development, starting with design conception and continue through final design obsolescence. The Stage-Gate method is essential in designing-in reliability capable of meeting consumers' expectations. In reliability economics it should ensure that a design (legislation) will meet the consumers' needs as it starts with an understanding of the full design requirements, economic environments, "hazardous greed conditions" (such as use and misuse, economic greed problems), potential design use and misuse, total design cost goals, and reliability service life needs.

Finally, to determine the level of effort associated with any policy, it typically should depend on whether it is a modification of a working policy, if it is a revolutionary one, or if it is a working policy with failure modes. The measure of risk needs to be explored to understand the policy development effort and cost. In general, there are different goals depending on if the policy is an existing one or a new design:

- Major goal of an existing design is
  - Reliability growth
  - Ensure reliability growth by finding and fixing failure modes through root cause analysis, design controls and corrective actions
- Major goal of a New Design
  - Ensure the design is reliable
  - Design-in reliability
  - Be proactive, not reactive

In order to facilitate the proposed DfR-E science, we suggest some initial basic economic reliability design rules (modified from reliability in industry):

- **Design Rule 1:** A reliability economic design should be able to withstand risky conditions, such as consumer use and abuse, economic greed, and terrorism to a reasonable extent.
- **Design Rule 2:** In order to fix fiscal failure modes of a design, root causes must first be properly identified and substantiated.
- **Design Rule 3:** Finding and fixing fiscal failure modes in an economic design is the only way to achieve reliability economic growth.
- **Design Rule 4:** Every economic design should require a FMEA be performed with a multi-disciplinary team in order to properly identify the FMEA factors and achieve agreement amongst the owners of the policy. Then design controls need investigation prior to corrective actions.

12

APPENDIX 2
FREE TRADE BASICS

We provide here an overview of tree trade and explain the trade deficit for the interested reader. This chapter provides the basic information on free trade in the U.S. Although it is not central to explaining the unjust nature of the trade deficit, we encourage readers to read this material.

12.1: Some Background Information on Free Trade and Job Outsourcing

Here we will present some background that looks at the benefits and historical failures of free trade as it exists today.

The basic principles of free trade from an economic theory are summarized in Remark 12.1.

Remark 12.1: "The underlying economic theory of free trade agreements is that of "comparative advantage," which originated in an 1817 book entitled *On the Principles of Political Economy and Taxation* by British political economist David Ricardo. Put simply, the "theory of comparative advantage" postulates that in a free marketplace, each country/area will ultimately specialize in that activity where it has comparative advantage (i.e. natural resources, skilled artisans, agriculture-friendly weather, etc.).... The result should be that all parties to the pact will increase their income." [209]

However, the increases in income can be narrowed down to a reduced number of individuals.

> **Remark 12.2:** "However, the theory refers only to aggregate wealth and says nothing about the distribution of wealth. In fact there may be significant losers, in particular among the recently protected industries with a comparative disadvantage. The proponents of free trade can, however, retort that the gains of the gainers exceed the losses of the losers."[210]

Some of the known benefits of free trade and job outsourcing are:

> **Remark 12.3:** 1) Low-priced goods, 2) reduced inflation due to maintaining low-priced products, 3) low-priced services, 4) new job opportunities in foreign-owned businesses, 5) new global opportunities in manufacturing, 6) imports/exports of agricultural goods and commodities, 7) export opportunities, 8) reduced likelihood of war with our trading partners due to foreign investors, and 9) manufacturing outsourcing raises the level of 3rd world countries.

> **Remark 12.4:** "In the 1980s, Milton Friedman, the Nobel Prize–winning economist and father of Monetarism, contended that some of the concerns of trade deficits are unfair criticisms in an attempt to push macroeconomic policies favorable to exporting industries. In the late 1970s and early 1980s, the U.S. had experienced high inflation and Friedman's policy positions tended to defend the stronger dollar at that time. He stated his belief that these trade deficits were not necessarily harmful to the economy at the time since the currency comes back to the country (country A sells to country B, country B sells to country C who buys from country A, but the trade deficit only includes A and B)." [211]

Unfortunately, Mr. Friedman may not have realized the extent of job losses and recognized the tax consequences of the trade deficit. He also like most economists, apparently never considered the ramifications of who pays for the trade deficit. This is really the concern of this book.

---

[209] http://usliberals.about.com/od/theeconomyjobs/i/FreeTradeAgmts.htm
[210] http://en.wikipedia.org/wiki/Free_trade_area
[211] http://en.wikipedia.org/wiki/Trade_deficit

In contrast to these benefits, there are a number of substantiated well-known current U.S. failures of free trade. From a reliability economics point of view, there are a number of free trade failure modes and their effects. We will briefly connect the dots to provide a bit more detail. They may be summarized:

Remark 12.5:
1) Significant problems exist for our current U.S. unemployment crisis due to job outsourcing that has occurred primarily in the manufacturing area (a decline of 31% since 1999).

2) Because of cheap foreign labor and lack of protectionism, the U.S. has lost its manufacturing base. This is well-known and a dominant challenge for America's unemployment problems and job creation problems.

3) U.S. corporation failures have occurred due to foreign competition that has had many advantages over U.S. businesses. For example, some foreign governments are accused of subsidizing products; they may pay for employee health insurance, and in general have cheaper labor. One industry that has been costly to America is the Detroit automakers. While they have had many mismanagement issues, the business structure was not able to survive the free trade competition. Japanese autos and other foreign imports have dominated our marketplace.

4) The U.S. now faces lost tax revenue due to a) layoffs and b) excess foreign profits. The excess lost tax revenue effectively <u>adds to the national debt</u>. This will cause cutbacks, difficulties with the national debt, and problems financing U.S. government–sponsored programs.

5) Because of the trade deficit with foreign countries we have also exported more dollars than we imported in foreign currency. These exported U.S. dollars held by foreigners must eventually find their way back and be reinvested into the U.S. The result is that more and more U.S. businesses are owned by foreign countries. In addition, foreign countries like China have also bought U.S. obligations so that, increasingly, national debt is owed to foreign countries. This also makes us politically beholden to countries like China, putting us in a weaker position to seek retribution on free-trade violations, as we will discuss below. This is also a key issue in this book (see Chapter 5).

6) There is a clear focus of wealth in free trade. Outsourcing allows for U.S. companies to exist with few or no actual manufacturing workers in the States. Businessmen can find free trade highly profitable, and this increases the separa-

tion of wealth in America, along with job losses. Studies indicate that the growing cost of globalization is a continued widening of the gap between the Haves and Have-Nots.[212]

The remark on item 4 about lost tax revenue is very relevant. It is now surfacing as a main issue for U.S. financial stability in the modern great recession and puts our economy at risk. The U.S. government appears to be its own worst enemy.

Remark 12.6: "Plunge in tax revenue worst since 1932—The recession is starving the government of tax revenue, just as the president and Congress are piling a major expansion of health care and other programs ….Tax receipts are on pace to drop 18 percent this year, the biggest single-year decline since the Great Depression, while the federal deficit balloons to a record $1.8 trillion. …Individual income tax receipts are down 22 percent from a year ago. Corporate income taxes are down 57 percent. Social Security tax receipts could drop for only the second time since 1940, and Medicare taxes are on pace to drop for only the third time ever." [213]

There are, of course, more failure modes and benefits of free trade. It could be a long controversial book. However, it is important to maintain focus on the key issues. In this regard let's start by reviewing the magnitude of the trade deficit. Table 12-1 provides the trade deficit to China, Japan, and NAFTA (Mexico, Canada) key trading partners. Total yearly deficit (all countries) is in last column.

Table 12-1 indicates that our biggest deficit in 2009 and 2010 exists with China (60% and 55%), followed by Mexico, and Japan. Note the last column totals $6.01 trillion for 11 years compared with an $8 trillion total since 1971, indicating that 75% of our trade deficit has occurred in just the last 11 years.

Warren Buffett has been quoted as saying,

Remark 12.7: "The U.S trade deficit is a bigger threat to the domestic economy than either the federal budget deficit or consumer debt and could lead to political turmoil... Right now, the rest of the world owns $3 trillion more of us than we own of them." [214]

---

[212] www.mapcruzin.com/news/news122000b.htm, "Growing Costs of Globalization: Wider Gaps Between Haves and Have-Nots by Year 2015, Says US Intelligence Report."
[213] www.denverpost.com/nationworld/ci_12986655
[214] http://en.wikipedia.org/wiki/Trade_deficit#Warren_Buffett_on_trade_deficits (January 2006)

Table 12-1 U.S. Trade Deficit Information in Billions of Dollars[215]

Year	Goods Only					China Percent of Total	U.S. Goods & Service Total Trade Deficit
	China	Japan	Mexico*	Canada*	Others		
2011	-$296	-$63	-$66	-$36	-$99	53%	-$558
2010	-$273	-$60	-$68	-$28	-$71	55%	-$500
2009	-$227	-$45	-$48	-$20	-$41	60%	-$381
2008	-$268	-$74	-$65	-$78	-$214	38%	-$699
2007	-$258	-$84	-$75	-$68	-$217	37%	-$702
2006	-$234	-$90	-$65	-$72	-$298	31%	-$759
2005	-$202	-$83	-$50	-$78	-$301	28%	-$714
2004	-$162	-$74	-$45	-$67	-$261	27%	-$609
2003	-$124	-$66	-$40	-$52	-$212	25%	-$494
2002	-$103	-$70	-$37	-$48	-$163	24%	-$421
2001	-$83	-$69	-$30	-$53	-$129	23%	-$364
2000	-$84	-$82	-$24	-$52	-$137	22%	-$379

*NAFTA Partner

Currently many companies are now recognizing that job outsourcing has gone too far, but still are unable to resolve their apparent need.

> **Remark 12.7-A:** July 2009, "Jeffery Immelt, the CEO of General Electric, recently said that 'the United States needs to invest in American manufacturing in order to get out of our current economic crisis. Some companies had gone overboard with outsourcing in the past and now it was time to bring that work back into the United States to create a strong economy.... GE plans to lead this effort.' The author of the article goes on to say that at the same time GE was actually shipping more jobs overseas by canceling U.S. orders to instead buying these parts from China."[216]

A historic overview of the trade deficit is depicted in Figure 12.1.

---

[215] www.census.gov/foreign-trade/balance/
[216] www.huffingtonpost.com/mike-elk/ge-promotes-manufacturing_b_241944.html, Author Mike Elk, huffington post on line.

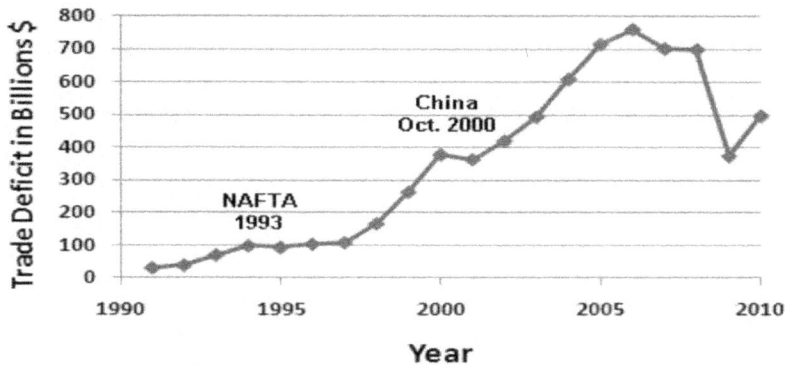

Figure 12-1 Trade deficits in goods and services - 1991 to 2010

There are many economists opposing free trade. NAFTA has been historically criticized for displacing U.S. jobs. Now China job losses are actually much worse from our trading policies.

Remark 12.8: "The High Price of "Free" Trade, November 17, 2003: Since the North American Free Trade Agreement (NAFTA) was signed in 1993, the rise in the U.S. trade deficit with Canada and Mexico through 2002 has caused the displacement of production that supported 879,280 U.S. jobs... Manufacturing industries were responsible for 78% of the net jobs lost under NAFTA, a total of 686,700 manufacturing jobs."[217]

Remark 12.8A: An Economic Policy Institute study claiming that the trade deficit with China cost more than 2.4 million U.S. jobs between 2001 and 2008[218]

Remark 12.9: "U.S. NAFTA Trade Deficit Surging Again Snapshot for November 5, 2003: The rise in the U.S. deficit with Canada and Mexico from 1993 to 2000 displaced production supported by 766,000 U.S. jobs. Most of those jobs would have been high-wage positions in manufacturing industries." [219]

Remark 12.9A Between NAFTA and China spanning 1993 and 2008 the total job outsourcing loss is at least 3.63 million. It is hard to assess lost tax revenue. One old economic study by a Harvard economist Martin Feldstein in 1971 estimated a tax loss of $10.61 per hour on even a $15 per hour job[220]. Using this underestimated value and providing an overestimate of displaced workers for 1 year of salary, the outsourcing cost to tax payers (2000 hr. work year) is ~ $77 billion. Us-

---

[217]www.policyarchive.org/bitstream/handle/10207/8113/epi_bp147.pdf?sequence=1

[218] http://online.wsj.com/article/BT-CO-20100323-713114.html?mod=WSJ_latestheadlines

[219]/www.epi.org/economic_snapshots/entry/webfeatures_snapshots_archive_11052003/

[220] http://www.econlib.org/library/Enc/Unemployment.html

ing a recent EPI estimate of about $700 week[221] including Cobra subsidies, the taxpayer cost is $131 billion. The GDP loss from consumer spending creating less product demand and affecting other layoffs is hard to factor. The EPI estimate is 8.4 million recent jobs lost. The cascade effect may be a factor of 10 with housing and bailout issues. This is ~$1 trillion in tax losses from the trade deficit effect.

Two recommended books criticizing Free Trade have received a lot of favorable attention.

> **Remark 12.10:** *The Myth of Free Trade: The Pooring of America*, by Ravi Batra "… The work outlines why America has become a debtor nation. The main cause is free trade. …Moreover, poor leadership has allowed foreign nations such as Japan, South Korea, and China to sing free trade's praises while following protectionist policies as tariffs, quotas, exchange controls and the like at home…We have become an open economy, the country has become awash with red ink in trade account."[222]

> **Remark 12.10A:** *Free Trade Doesn't Work,* by Ian Fletcher, "Presents the failures of an unrestrained trade system and offers up a balanced discussion of what a managed trade system could accomplish in its place. His discussion of the WTO goals, and of China's open defiance of the spirit of WTO rules, is refreshingly honest and timely…"[167]

12.2: Trade Deficit, National Debt, and U.S. Currency

Trade deficit means foreigners increasingly own U.S. dollars. For example, when the U.S. spends $10 on imports from China and China only ends up spending $5 on imports from the U.S., China has a $5 U.S. gain. China's currency is the yuan (about 6.8 yuan equals 1 U.S. dollar as of September 2009). Therefore it has two choices: sell the dollar for the yuan, which could decrease the value of the dollar, or purchase securities such as U.S. stocks or treasury bonds. Since treasury bonds are, in essence, loans to the U.S. government, the trade deficit and the trading partners of the U.S. fund some of the national debt. The vast majority of the national debt is held by Americans. However, foreigners own about $3.5 trillion of our $14 trillion–plus debt.

Foreigners in 2010 have been happy to hold onto U.S. securities. The concern is that at some point, foreigners may want to reduce their holdings. If this occurs rapidly, it could send the value of the dollar, U.S. stocks, and bond prices plunging, since the government will have to print money to pay back the foreign countries. This poses a risk. The current foreign holdings of the U.S. debt are listed in Table 12-2. We see there is strong correlation to the trade deficit. That is, China, Japan, and oil exporters are the largest holders of our debt and proportionately the largest countries that we have a trade

---

[221] http://www.epi.org/publications/entry/jobs_crisis_fact_sheet/
[222] www.amazon.com/reviews

deficit with. It is also a cause for concern that, because China and oil exporters hold so much of our debt, many consider their interests unfriendly.

Remark 12.11: In February 2009—an article entitled "Did 2008's $677 Billion Trade Deficit Cause The Recession?" was posted by the economist Peter Morici, who noted that the Chinese government holds about $2 trillion in U.S. and other securities and he worries if we add that to the holdings of Middle East sovereigns and royal families, that the potential purchases of U.S. businesses by foreigners unfriendly to the U.S. is alarming. He believes the trade deficit is a root cause to the recession.[223]

Table 12-2 U.S. Debt Owned by Foreigners and Related Trade Deficit[224]

Nation	Dec. 2010[225] Foreign-Owned U.S. Treasuries in Billions of Dollars	Treasuries Owned in Percentage	2000-2010 Cum. U.S. Trade Deficit in Billions[226]
China	1,160.10	26.10%	2,018
Japan	882.3	19.90%	797
United Kingdom	272.1	6.10%	
Oil exporters[1]	211.9	4.80%	NA
Brazil	186.1	4.20%	
Caribbean Banking Centers[2]	168.6	3.80%	
Hong Kong (Special Administrative Region)	134.2	3.00%	
Switzerland	107	2.40%	
Taiwan	155.1	3.50%	
Russia	151	3.40%	
Subtotal of top 10 holders	3,428.40	77.20%	
Grand Total	4,439.60	100.00%	

[1]Saudi Arabia, Venezuela, Libya, Iran, Iraq, the United Arab Emirates, Bahrain, Kuwait, Oman, Qatar, Ecuador, Indonesia, Algeria, Gabon, and Nigeria
[2]Bahamas, Bermuda, Cayman Islands, Netherlands Antilles, British Virgin Islands and Panama

---

[223] http://seekingalpha.com/article/120195-did-2008-s-677-billion-trade-deficit-cause-the-recessio
[224] http://en.wikipedia.org/wiki/United_States_public_debt
[225] ttp://en.wikipedia.org/wiki/United_States_public_debt
[226] www.census.gov/foreign-trade/top/dst/current/deficit.html

To put this matter in perspective, Table 12-2 provides information on U.S. debt owed to foreigners.

Foreigners not only own U.S. debt, but also buy U.S. businesses. America is now for sale to foreigners because of the trade deficit, which also hurts tax revenues.

> **Remark 12.11-A** Aug. 08 - "American icons (now owned by foreigners) such as storied brewer Anheuser-Busch Companies Inc and the landmark Chrysler Building in New York....According to the Grant Thornton report...."[227]

Foreign owners often replace American workers when they buy U.S businesses. The net job increase to jobs lost is fractional[228]. Below is an interesting excerpt regarding a U.S company purchased by a German company. The lack of sensible reliability economics is concerning in U.S free trade policy.

> **Remark 12.11-B:** "As the American employees were leaving the company for one reason or another, they were being replaced by German employees. Also, as new positions were opened, most of the positions were filled with; who else but German individuals. 6 years after the buy-out of the American firm, the ratio of the American employees vs. German employees has increased to around 50/50...."[229]

Free trade advocates feel that foreign reinvestments create lots of job opportunities. Yet a quick investigation doesn't seem to indicate a reasonable percentage compared to what is being invested.

> **Remark 12.11C:** Aug, 2008 – "According to the Grant Thornton report, total assets at foreign-owned companies increased 15 percent to $9.2 trillion in 2005 from $8.0 trillion a year earlier and was more than three times the 1996 total of $3 trillion. Foreign-owned assets totaled just $37 billion in 1971...."[230]
>
> **Remark 12.11D:** "Foreign-owned companies in the United States have a work force of more than 5.3 million, or some 3.5% of all workers."[231]

According to 12.11C and D, foreigners own 15% of U.S. companies but only employ 3.5%. Extrapolating to 100%, the employment would only be 25%! Current estimate of foreign ownership is $6.9 trillion in businesses and $3 trillion in treasuries totaling $9.9 trillion. U.S. business net worth is about $50 trillion (~13.9%). The total trade deficit is $7.5 trillion. About 76% of the ownership is due to the deficit. At the mean rate of

---

[227]www.reuters.com/article/domesticNews/idUSN2744743020080827

[228] http://www.aflcio.org/issues/jobseconomy/jobs/outsourcing_myths.cfm

[229]www.commentaryusa.com/commentary/economy/do-foreigners-care-for-the-u.s.-economy.html

[230] http://www.reuters.com/article/idUSN2744743020080827

[231] www.nytimes.com/2009/10/18/business/18excerpt.html

$0.55 trillion/yr. (in Table 9.2), half the U.S. businesses could be foreign owned in just 65 years (using 50% profit model invested in U.S. businesses); this ownership is mostly by China!

12.3: Root Cause Discussion
In this section we provide information on the root causes.

12.3.1: Root Cause—High- Versus Low-Wage Economies
The key root cause is primarily high-wage versus low-wage economies. This implies that whenever a low-wage country trades with a high-wage country it will create big losers and winners. One macroeconomic book explained this concept as follows:

> **Remark 12.12:** "Trade between high-wage countries tends to be a modest win for all, or almost all, concerned....By contrast, trade between countries at very different levels of economic development tends to create large classes of losers as well as winners....And the biggest growth of imports has come from countries with very low wages....South Korea, Taiwan, Hong Kong and Singapore paid wages of 25 percent of U.S. levels in 1990. Since then however, the sources of our imports have shifted to Mexico, where wages are 11 percent of the U.S. level, and China, where they're only 3 or 4 percent....[232]"

A simple theory will be provided that we will call "the law of financial trade deficit equilibrium."

> **Remark 12.13: Law of Financial Trade Deficit Equilibrium**—Consider two containers separated by a wall, one having a high concentration of air, and one with very little air. Once the wall is removed, due to the pressure and concentration difference, after a period of time both containers will have the same amount of air, thus reaching equilibrium. In a similar manner, if two economies have free cash flow, such as China (considered a developing country) and the U.S., the currencies will flow towards financial equilibrium (from richer country to poorer). The imbalanced monetary pressure causing excess deficit is due mainly to three key trade deficit reasons: cost of wages, each country's GDP, and the value of the country's currency.

In our analogy, we might consider the point where the free trade "concentration wall" was officially removed between the U.S. and China to have occurred when President Clinton signed a bill extending permanent, normal trade status to China on October 10, 2000. This bill clearly undercut American and Mexican factory workers. In terms of

---

[232] *Principles of Macroeconomics*, N. Gregory Mankiw, 5th edition, 2009 South-Western Cengage Learning, PP 192-193.

free trade, this was a severe final attack on American factory workers. As Remark 12.12 notes, wages in China were almost a quarter of that for the Mexican worker. Since that point in time, in accordance with Remark 12.13, the high concentration of cash has flowed to the low concentration, as noted by our enormous imbalance with the trade deficit that peaked at $760 billion in 2006 (see Table 12-1). This is now magnified by the fact that, as we stated earlier, in roughly nine short years, the U.S. has ended up owing China over $800 billion through China's purchase of U.S. treasuries.

It is important to realize the relationship between GDP (Gross Domestic Product) and the population size:

> **Remark 12.14:** "In order for Americans to maintain their standard of living, GDP needs to grow at least as fast as the population!"[233]

Here, GDP is a measure of the size of our economy from everyone's total income. To put this a bit more in perspective, Tables 12-3 and 12-4 provide statistics of the population growth and GDP information from 2000 to 2008 for China and U.S.

Table 12-3 China's Overall Population and GDP Growth from 2000 to 2008[234]

Year	China Population (Billions)	Pop Growth Since 2000	Adjusted Pop Growth Rate	GDP per Capita China in U.S. dollars	Real GDP* Growth Rate %	Billions GDP China
2000	1.26	0.00%	0.9%	$3,800	7%	4800
2001	1.27	0.88%	0.88%	$3600	8%	4500
2002	1.28	1.75%	0.87%	$4600	8%	6000
2003	1.29	2.35%	0.6%	$4400	8%	5700
2004	1.30	2.92%	0.57%	$5000	9.1%	6449
2005	1.31	3.50%	0.58%	$5600	9.1%	7262
2006	1.31	4.09%	0.59%	$6800	10.2%	8883
2007	1.32	4.70%	0.61%	$7700	10.7%	10170
2008	1.33	5.33%	0.63%	$5400	11.9%	7099
2009	1.34	5.99%	0.66%	$4900	9%	6473

From Tables 12-3 and 12-4, our population consisted of about 304 million, while China's population consisted of 1,330 million in 2008. China, in 2008, had over four times as many consumers. Noting this, we see that China's GDP skyrocketed in this timeframe from 7% to 11.4% since the Free Trade Bill was passed between the U.S. and China. In comparison, the U.S. GDP growth rate ended down from 4.1% to 2.2% according to the source CIA World Factbook (Tables 12-3 and 12-4).

---

[233] http://truecostblog.com/2008/01/25/gdp-doesnt-matter-gdp-per-capita-does/
[234] CIA World Factbook—as of January 1, 2009, www.indexmundi.com/g/g.aspx?v=67&c=ch&l=en

Table 12-4 U.S. Overall Population and GDP Growth from 2000 to 2008[235]

Year	U.S. Pop (Billions)	U.S. Pop Growth Since 2000	Adjusted Pop Growth Rate	U.S. GDP Per Capita in dollars	U.S. GDP in Billions	Real GDP* Growth Rate %
2000	0.276	0.0%	0.91%	$33,900	9,255	4.1%
2001	0.278	0.9%	0.9%	$36,200	9,963	5%
2002	0.281	1.79%	0.89%	$36,300	10,082	0.3%
2003	0.290	2.71%	0.92%	$37,600	10,400	2.45%
2004	0.293	3.63%	0.92%	$37,800	10,990	3.1%
2005	0.296	4.55%	0.92%	$40,100	11,750	4.4%
2006	0.298	5.46%	0.91%	$41,600	12,310	3.2%
2007	0.301	6.35%	0.894%	$44,000	13,130	3.2%
2008	0.304	7.24%	0.883%	$45,800	13,780	2.1%
2009	0.307	8.21%	0.975%	$46,300	13,820	1.1%

One should also note that this is an inversion with our population growth compared to China. That is, China's population grew by 5.4% and their GDP by 4.4% since 2000. In contrast, the U.S. GDP growth rate contracted -1.9% while its population grew 10.3% since 2000. The World CIA Factbook defines the GDP growth on an annual basis adjusted for inflation and expressed as a percent. (The reader might note that the U.S. GDP and GDP per capita did increase from 2000 to 2008. Therefore, statistics in this regard must be reviewed from this source on the GDP growth rate.) However, it is clear that China's GDP is growing faster than the U.S., while America's population appears to be growing faster than China's.

It is also important to realize that cash flow is impacted by the average income per person (this is GDP per capita). By comparison, it was $46,000 for the U.S. citizens compared to $5,300 for Chinese citizens in 2008.

Remark 12.15: "While GDP measures the size of the total economy, it's GDP per capita, the slice of GDP that an "average" American has that really matters. While GDP per capita doesn't take into account income inequality and other measures...."[236]

---

[235]CIA World Factbook—as of January 1, 2009, www.indexmundi.com/g/g.aspx?v=67&c=ch&l=en

[236] http://truecostblog.com/2008/01/25/gdp-doesnt-matter-gdp-per-capita-does/

So although China has four times as many consumers, we had on average a factor of 8.7 times higher incomes in 2008. This fact helps us to understand some of the trade imbalance. This is really the root cause issue; we are a high-income wage earning country trading with a low-income country. Logically, the cash flow is eventually going to get distributed. Financially, it means that the U.S. is giving up quite a bit in the name of free trade and will continue to do so until the playing field is leveled. Since China is our largest trading partner, this fact implies that the U.S. must reduce its population, grow its GDP at a faster rate, reduce the cost of living and wage earnings, or continue to face the economic crisis that is now occurring.

On the positive side, since China's GDP is growing faster than that of the U.S., eventually the trade deficiency should come down as the value of their currency strengthens compared to the U.S. This is related to the theory of free trade, where eventually the U.S. currency will weaken; exports should then increase to bring back the trade imbalance.

> **Remark 12.16:** "As the yuan appreciates, the relative prices of Chinese-produced goods to American businesses and consumers will rise, reducing U.S. demand for Chinese imports. Simultaneously, the relative prices of U.S. products to Chinese purchasers will decrease, allowing U.S. exports to rise. At least, that is the theory."[237]

This, in theory, is how free trade should work. However, eventually when China has some measure of financial equilibrium with the U.S., the U.S. GDP per capita, according to our law of financial free trade equilibrium, must be significantly reduced simply due to the combined effect of our two populations.

So it would appear the assumption is somewhat flawed. There are also other problems with conducting free trade fairly as we have noted. This has occurred with both China and Japan.

---

[237] www.freetrade.org/node/83

13

APPENDIX 3
CITIZENS FOR EQUAL TRADE SIGNED PETITION

Stop Trade Deficit Massive Job & Tax Losses
It's Unconstitutional!

This book has periodic updates; if you sign this petition, your name will likely appear in the next version

To sign go to: www.CitizensForEqualTrade.org and click on sign petition

Target: Dear U.S. Congress Member and Supreme Court:

Sponsored by: Citizens For Equal Trade

We the undersigned, call for a policy of equal trade to stop U.S. large trade deficits (i.e., where imports greatly exceed exports). Most U.S. products now come from foreign countries which have cost over 3.6 million U.S. jobs losses. These lost jobs mean the U.S. government cannot collect taxes on lost wages, during unemployment, causing tax problems and more government debt. This escalates the national debt and is unconstitutional (explained in the appendix). Many other reasons for tax losses are also in the appendix. Citizens For Equal Trade estimates roughly $1 trillion in lost U.S. taxes since 1971 due to *excessive* trade deficits and foreign cheating. On our website it is demonstrated that tax losses would be stopped if equal trade were U.S. policy. This provides further evidence that only equal trade is ethical, constitutional, and fair.

Additionally foreigners reinvest much of their yearly huge profits from the trade deficit by buying up U.S. businesses. Foreigners now own 23% of U.S. businesses, but actually only employ about 3.7% of the U.S. workforce. This poor job creation means higher unemployment, more lost wages and less tax revenue, and even more national debt. In also means we are beholden to foreigners (mainly China) as they increase U.S. ownership yearly.

We call for the following:

1)   Government economists provide estimates of the actual tax losses that occur due to the trade deficit.

2)   The U.S. Supreme court rule on the constitutionality of the trade deficit effects with its related tax losses which violates Article 1, Section 9, Clause 5 (see appendix). U.S. citizens refuse to keep subsidizing trade deficit foreign imports through U.S. tax losses with massive lost jobs.

3)   Congress transition from a policy of free trade to equal trade by seriously considering the Balance Trade Restoration Act of 2006 (that was never voted on) or a similar equal trade act.

Petition Appendix

(Please see CitizensForEqualTrade.Org for more full explanations)

Table 13-1 Citizens for Equal Trade Sample Signatures

No.	Date Signed	First Name	Last Name	City	State/Pro vince	Coun- try	Has your job been outsourced? How do you feel about the trade deficit?
1	5/11/2 010	Alec	Feinberg	Fort Collins	Colorado	U.S.A.	
2	5/13/2 010	Linda	Feinberg	Fort Collins	Colorado	U.S.A.	I agree, the trade deficit is ruining the U.S.
3	5/13/2 010	Ri- chard	Feinberg	Chestnut Hill	Massa- chusetts	U.S.A.	I agree with this petition and don't under- stand today's economists who support free trade.
4	5/14/2 010	STEVE	KLEIN	Herndon	Virginia	U.S.A.	Has your job been outsourced? How do you feel about the trade deficit?
5	5/14/2 010	Steve	miller	Greer	South Carolina	U.S.A.	

No.	Date Signed	First Name	Last Name	City	State/Province	Country	Has your job been outsourced? How do you feel about the trade deficit?
6	5/14/2010	Courtney	Cobbs	North Little Rock	Arkansas	U.S.A.	There are plenty of jobs the U.S. can have if we stopped outsourcing jobs to China, Mexico, Thailand, etc.
7	5/14/2010	Grady	Gjovik	lake bluff	Illinois	U.S.A.	I have lost my job due to "Free Trade" outsourcing. Nafta/Cafta/WTO free trade has destroyed America's middle class. Repeal free trade.
8	5/14/2010	Norma	Ellison	findlay	Ohio	U.S.A.	
9	5/15/2010	Dale	Catanzaro	Homosassa	Florida	U.S.A.	The trade deficit in this country is abominable. It is the corporate and goverm,emt elite who benifit
10	5/16/2010	Marissa	Feinberg	New York	New York	U.S.A.	
11	5/17/2010	Dick	Thomson	Chicago	Illinois	U.S.A.	A nation is defined by its trade and immigration barriers. Without tariffs on the importation of goods and labor, parity pricing for agricultural and mineral production, and a rising standard of living, the United States is no more than a temporary paddock for the money-changers to graze their flock. Money is worse than useless when it's not a reflection of the production of real wealth. Let's get educated, elect representatives who understand American traditions, and kill free trade.
12	5/17/2010	Andy	Gussert	Madison	Wisconsin	U.S.A.	Ask your Congressional member to support the TRADE Act.
13	5/17/2010	Bennett	Tramer	Santa Monica	California	U.S.A.	
14	5/18/2010	Jennifer	Feinberg	Fort Collins	Colorado	U.S.A.	
15	5/19/2010	Jean	Lord	Cliffwood Bch	New Jersey	U.S.A.	
16	5/19/2010	ROGER	SIDELL	Orlando	Florida	U.S.A.	
17	5/19/2010	Mark	Silver	East Harford	Connecticut	U.S.A.	
18	5/19/2010	Beverly	Sllver	east hartford	Connecticut	U.S.A.	
19	5/23/2010	pamela	veenendaal	Fort Collins Co	Colorado	U.S.A.	
20	5/23/2010	jan	veenendaal	Fort Collins Co	Colorado	U.S.A.	
21	5/23/2010	kayla	veenendaal	Fort Collins Co	Colorado	U.S.A.	
22	5/23/2010	caitlin	veenendaal	Fort Collins Co	Colorado	U.S.A.	

No.	Date Signed	First Name	Last Name	City	State/Province	Country	Has your job been outsourced? How do you feel about the trade deficit?
23	5/30/2010	deanna	kline	kansas city	Missouri	U.S.A.	
24	5/30/2010	Lou	Rosenberg	Fort Collins	Colorado	U.S.A.	
25	5/30/2010	Sharon	Rosenberg	Fort Collins	Colorado	U.S.A.	
26	5/30/2010	Judy	Coleman	Omaha	Nebraska	U.S.A.	We must take care of ourselves.
27	5/31/2010	Frank	Gerry	Dona Vista	Florida	U.S.A.	
28	6/6/2010	SHIRLEY	BABA	Scotland		United Kingdom	
29	6/13/2010	Harriet	Stucke	Philadelphia	Pennsylvania	U.S.A.	Things have gotten so out of hand that I wonder if we can ever make it right again. I personally feel that the industry that sends their work to China, should also be made to live in China. This way maybe they would think twice about outsourcing the work.
30	6/13/2010	Helen T	Mosley	Bayside	New York	U.S.A.	
31	6/13/2010	Michael	Tolbert	Tyler	Texas	U.S.A.	It should be clear to all by now that we can not sustain our current above average standard of living with half trillion dollar trade deficits ear after year. Please take action to protect the future of our nation by demanding that all foreign trade partners adhere to fair trade laws.
32	6/13/2010	Virgil	Alley	Aurora	Missouri	U.S.A.	Anyone with any common sense should realize when people are working they pay taxes far more than when they are drawing unemployment.Also when they have more money they buy more goods and services.Sure would be nice if more of the products they purchased was MADE IN USA.
33	6/13/2010	Ellen	Hammond	Woodburn	Oregon	U.S.A.	We need th jobs sent oversea returned to the U.S. If the companies that don't want to abide by our rules then they shoulc be forbidden to have thier products come to the U.S. We can get along without them.
34	6/13/2010	Robert	Bright	West Hollywood	California	U.S.A.	Save the middle class! Stop so-called free trade, give us equal trade!
35	6/13/2010	Mary	Ebbert	Wheeling	West Virginia	U.S.A.	Our once thriving steel plants are now Russian owned, and operating at less than 10% capacity. Which affected the coal mines and transportation. Unemployment is above national figures. HELP!

No.	Date Signed	First Name	Last Name	City	State/Province	Country	Has your job been outsourced? How do you feel about the trade deficit?
36	6/13/2010	Terresa	Newport	Sandy	Utah	U.S.A.	
37	6/13/2010	Bruce	Morgan	Riverside	California	U.S.A.	
38	6/14/2010	ROBERT	WIMER	HOWELL	Michigan	U.S.A.	
39	6/14/2010	Dave	Corbin	San Jose	California	U.S.A.	Congress needs to figure out a way to tax the salaries of foreign workers being used by US Corporations, whether it's direct salaries or funds paid to foreign companies that replace functions formerly done within the US companies i.e customer service, accounting IT or whatever. This would help reduce the deficit as well as level the playing field and discourage outsourcing.
40	6/15/2010	Corey	Mondello	Boston	Massachusetts	U.S.A.	
41	7/14/2010	D	T	Woonsocket	Rhode Island	U.S.A.	The Free Trade is about Foreign Greed and our Government's failure to look out for Americaâ€™s interest.
42	7/31/2010	hector	martinez	riverview	Florida	U.S.A.	we want our country back
43	8/22/2010	Ken	Barnes	Portland	Oregon	U.S.A.	
44	8/23/2010	Holly	Bachman	Bechtelsville	Pennsylvania	U.S.A.	
45	8/24/2010	Nate	Ciambor	Niceville	Florida	U.S.A.	
46	9/7/2010	Paula	Baumann	Ellwangen		Germany	
47	9/10/2010	stephen	turlo	victorville	California	U.S.A.	
48	10/1/2010	Timothy	Bal	Belle Mead	New Jersey	U.S.A.	I have opposed the false ideology of "free trade" for several decades. It is the biggest cause of our present economic problems. This Great Recession is very different from the Great Depression. (The latter was caused by the gold standard. The current problem is "free trade".)
49	10/12/2010	Christopher	Kilcullen	Evergreen	Colorado	U.S.A.	
50	10/16/2010	Claire	Sayers	Pound Ridge	New York	U.S.A.	
51	11/29/2010	Pam	Boland	Grovetown	Georgia	U.S.A.	
52	12/1/2010	Glenn	Swanson	Everett	Washington	U.S.A.	
53	12/1/2010	James	Weil	Glendale	California	U.S.A.	

No.	Date Signed	First Name	Last Name	City	State/Province	Country	Has your job been outsourced? How do you feel about the trade deficit?
54	12/1/2010	Gail	Williams	Vancouver	Washington	U.S.A.	
55	12/2/2010	Ruby	Lam	Brooklyn Park	Maryland	U.S.A.	
56	12/9/2010	sherri	blakeley	Grants Pass	Oregon	U.S.A.	The Trade Deficit is a part of the "Twin Deficit" problem facing the U.S. and is discussed little and next to none compared to the Annual Deficit and the National Debt. It is my understanding too, the the disparity between imports and exports, or the fact that we consume more than we produce leads to more borrowing to make up for this loss. We are increasingly as a nation aware of, and are dealing with, the harsh realities of our mounting debt and an unprecedented economic crisis that must take into consideration all our debt if we are to successfully resolve the situation effectively and to our satisfaction. A balanced trade policy seems obvious if we are to have a balanced budget in the future. Please consider Citizens for Equal Trade's solutions and insights, and lets bring about change we all can believe in.
57	12/26/2010	Jaciel	Tamez	West Bend	Wisconsin	U.S.A.	The trade deficit is a serious concern. As a United States Citizen, I have often wondered why this problem has been ignored by our government for so long. Jaciel Tamez
58	12/27/2010	Henry	Stowe	Sanford	Florida	U.S.A.	
59	12/28/2010	Martin	Thomas	Liberty	Kentucky	U.S.A.	
60	1/23/2011	luz	maldonado	davie	Florida	U.S.A.	I Think what's happening to the American citizens is wrong we are turning to a third world country
61	2/3/2011	Wendy	Castilone	Citrus Heights	California	U.S.A.	Yes! I work for HP and thousands of jobs, including many of my co-workers and friends, were outsourced since 2000.
62	2/6/2011	Wanda	S. Ballentine	Eagan	Minnesota	U.S.A.	
63	2/8/2011	Paula	Jacobs	Corpus Christi	Texas	U.S.A.	
64	3/13/2011	Jean L.	Corcoran	Tarpon Springs	Florida	U.S.A.	
65	3/19/2011	Erin	Harris	Albuquerque	New Mexico	U.S.A.	
69	7/26/2011	Stephen	McDowel	San Diago	CA	U.S.A.	God bless this petition

See more signatures at our petition sight.

List of Tables

List of Figures

---

[238] 2007 Graphical data: www.bea.gov/newsreleases/international/intinv/2008/pdf/intinv07.pdf

Some Recommended Trade Reform Sources

Please join and support:
- *Coalition for a Prosperous America (CPA)*
- *Citizens Trade Campaign*

Please sign our petition at:
- *Citizens for Equal Trade.org*

Trade Reform Web sources:
- *www.Citizensforequaltrade.org,*
- *Coalition for a Prosperous America (CPA) websites: www.prosperousamerica.org, and www.TradeReform.org,*
- *Citizens Trade website: Citizenstrade.org,*
- *www.Americaneconomicalert.org,*
- *www.economyincrisis.org*

Trade Reform Books:
- *Trade Deficit Destroying America From Illegal and Unconstitutional Effects Dr. Alec Feinberg*
- *The Truth of the Modern Recession, Dr. Alec Feinberg*
- *Free Trade Doesn't Work: What Should Replace It and Why, Ian Fletcher*
- *Death by China: Confronting the Dragon – A Global Call to Action, Peter Navarro and Greg Autry*
- *The Myth of Free Trade: The Pooring of America, Dr. Ravi Batra*
- *Trading Away Our Future, R. Richman, H. Richman, J. Richman*

Buy America Websites:
- *AmericanMadeMatters.com*
- *AmericansWorking.com*
- *AmericasGotProduct.com*
- *MadeinUSA.org*

Index of Key Testimonies by Economists

Section 3.1.2: Collaborative MIT Study.

Section 3.1.2.3: 1) Tax breaks for multinational corporations, 2) Deferral taxation of multinational corporations' tax shelter law.

Section 3.2.1: Reverse tariff trade deficit tax violates U.S. Constitutional law. Reference herein provides discussion with constitutional law professor.

Section 4.1.1: An empirical analysis of the relationship between the budget deficit and the trade deficit, 1960-2003.

Section 4.1.2: U.S. trade deficit creates budget deficit –NAFTA and China causality study, 1994-2007.

Section 4.2.1: Correlation analysis –trade deficit and national debt.

Section 5.2: Foreign ownership of U.S. companies 51% by 2033 with skyrocketing U.S. unemployment projected.

Section 5.3: Analysis of Internal Revenue Service data, Grant Thornton Report.

Section 6.2.2: Patent, Copyright and Trademark Piracy, Testimony of Former Senator Gordon – China largest offender.

Section 6.3.1: Japan's currency manipulation helps topple U.S. auto industry and Detroit jobs.

Section 6.3.2: China's unmatched VAT tax – A comparative advantage.

Section 7.1: Trade deficit countries have higher unemployment. Higher unemployment is a key tax burden to U.S. revenues.

Section 7.1, 6.1.1: Currency manipulation cost 2.1 of 3 million lost trade deficit jobs.

Section 8.1: Redistributing lower and middle class wealth to upper class Americans and foreigners.

HOW YOU CAN HELP

After reading this book, please forward it to your Congressperson so they can learn the facts. Discuss these facts with your representative and radio talk show host. Please sign our petition at CitizensForEqualTrade.org. If you are a lawyer and have means, consider threatening a Supreme Court action to help alarm congress.

NOTES

About the Author

Dr. Alec Feinberg is also the author of the multi-award winning book, *The Truth of the Modern Recession*. This book is written in conjunction with Citizens for Equal Trade.

Alec holds a Ph.D. in Physics as well as minors in mathematics and statistics. He has over 30 years experience in industrial statistics and reliability analysis. He is author of three books: one on industrial reliability entitled <u>Design for Reliability</u>, and two on reliability economics - <u>The Truth of the Modern Recession</u> and most recently, this book. Alec is also the inventor of Reliability Economics a political economic bipartisan solution as discussed in these books. He is founder of Citizens for Equal Trade (CET) which seeks to educate the public and petition against the devastating impact of the trade deficit. CET has numerous published articles on the trade deficit effects. This book features much of the related research that was done for these articles.

CET Articles:
1. Dollar and Euro Free Trade Violations Cost Millions of Global jobs (September 26, 2011) in economyincrisis.org
2. Currency Manipulation Cost 2.1 of 3 Million Lost Trade Deficit Jobs (June 2, 2011), in economyincrisis.org and www.tradereform.org
3. Foreign Ownership of U.S. Companies Rising: Foreign Ownership of U.S. Companies 51% by 2033 with Skyrocketing U.S. Unemployment Projected due to the Trojan Horse Trade Deficit (March 10, 2011), in economyincrisis.org and www.tradereform.org
4. Trade Deficit Now Forces $900 Billion Stimulus – Your U.S. Reverse Tariff for 2011 (January 11, 2011), in economyincrisis.org and www.tradereform.org
5. CET Seeks Help to Challenge Legality of the U.S. Trade Deficit (Dec. 1, 2010) http://economyincrisis.org/content/cet-seeks-help-challenge-legality-us-trade-deficit
6. Free Trade Under Fire" is Irresponsibly Written – Book Review (Oct. 18, 2010), in economyincrisis.org and www.tradereform.org
7. How to Fix the Economy, Experts Ignore the U.S. Trade Deficit (Oct. 7, 2010), in economyincrisis.org and www.tradereform.org
8. Trade Deficit Countries Have Higher Unemployment Rates–Balanced Trade is Needed, (Sept. 29, 2010), in economyincrisis.org and www.tradereform.org
9. Trade Deficit is Illegal, Unconstitutional… (Sept. 9, 2010), in economyincrisis.org
10. Trade Deficit's Reverse Tariff Increased the U.S. National Debt – an 84% Correlation! (Aug. 19 2010), in economyincrisis.org and www.tradereform.org
11. Reverse Tariff - Economic Crisis Due to Free Trade's Flaw (Aug. 2, 2010), in economyincrisis.org and www.tradereform.org
12. Biggest Threat to America's Future --The U.S. Trade Deficit (June 14, 2010), in economyincrisis.org and www.tradereform.org